Pattern
From
Proverbs 31

Pattern From Proverbs 31

Sharon Rhoades

Regular Baptist Press
1300 North Meacham Road
Post Office Box 95500
Schaumburg, Illinois 60195

Efforts to locate sources of some quotes have been unsuccessful.

Library of Congress Cataloging-in-Publication Data

Rhoades, Sharon, 1945-
    Pattern from Proverbs 31.

    Bibliography: p.
    1. Women—Biblical teaching. 2. Bible. O.T.
Proverbs XXXI—Criticism, interpretation, etc.
I. Title
BS1199.W7R47 1985   242'.643   85-14486
ISBN 0-87227-101-3

Pattern from Proverbs 31
© 1985
Regular Baptist Press
Schaumburg, Illinois
Printed in U.S.A.

Dedicated lovingly to my mother Berniece Groves, who demonstrates the pattern qualities of God's ideal woman.

CONTENTS

CONTENTS

INTRODUCTION

The book of Proverbs arose out of an immediate, local setting, involving people and their relationships to each other and God. The common title of the book is "Proverbs" from the opening phrase, "The proverbs of Solomon" in verse 1, chapter 1. Matthew Henry's *Commentary on the Whole Bible* says, "The Hebrew word for proverbs is 'mashal' and comes from the word that signifies 'to rule' or 'have dominion' because of the commanding power and influence which wise and weighty sayings have on men. These proverbs of Solomon are not merely a collection of the wise sayings, but the dictates of the Spirit of God in Solomon."[1]

Most of the proverbs originated with Solomon, son of King David. This work is dated around 950-900 B.C. Solomon was a unique individual in many ways. He was a very rich king and his dominions were very large; he was a king of great influence. However, Solomon gave assent to the duty of divine things. His wisdom was a direct gift from God (1 Kings 3:5-12). He is the author of 3,000 proverbs and 1,005 songs (1 Kings 4:32).

Solomon is the author of three Old Testament books of the Bible. One commentator, John Phillips, suggests the possibility of the books being written at different stages of Solomon's life: Song of Solomon, written when he was young and in love; Proverbs, written when he was middle-aged, when his intellectual powers were at their peak; Ecclesiastes, written in his old age, when he was disappointed and disillusioned with the carnality of much of his life.[2]

The writings of Proverbs and Psalms took place about the same time. David's psalms give a vivid view of worship by God's people before the decline of the kingdom. Solomon's proverbs reflect the zealous concern of believers for a righteous walk. The

Psalms teach how to get along with God and the Proverbs teach how to get along with others.

The Proverbs are God's detailed instructions and exhortations to His people concerning their thought-and-deed life. The Proverbs are mainly about personal ethics, not as the sinner's way to God, but as the believer's walk with God on this earth. Though the book is not intended to elaborate on the way of salvation, such key phrases as "the fear (reverence or awe) of the Lord" tell basically how a sinner is brought into fellowship with God. The counsel of Proverbs is profitable for all people, saved and unsaved; however, the unsaved cannot claim salvation by doing the good deeds written in Proverbs (Eph. 2:8, 9). The "wise" man of Proverbs is the righteous man, and no man is righteous unless he is clothed with the righteousness of Christ. So the truly wise person today is the person who has a personal relationship with Jesus Christ as a born-again Christian (John 3:3).

The key word throughout Proverbs is *wisdom.* "The fear of the Lord is the beginning of knowledge: but fools despise wisdom and instruction" (Prov. 1:7). The Hebrew word for wisdom is *chokmah.* Wisdom does not simply mean knowledge. It is interpreted as righteousness or holiness, which describes the heart of that person who truly knows God. Likewise, "fool" and "folly" are interpreted as meaning wickedness of the person who does not have a personal relationship with Jesus Christ.

In the Old Testament, "knowledge" means information or eternal truth. "Wisdom" refers to skill. Wisdom is indicated in Proverbs 1:2-4. This wisdom is not mere head knowledge but divinely enlightened understanding of what is evil (1 Kings 3:9) and a personal experiential knowledge of the Lord (Eccles. 12:9-14; 2 Tim. 3:16).[3]

The fear of the Lord is the beginning of knowledge and wisdom. This is the starting point. Fools despise wisdom and instruction. Individuals must choose either to live in the power of God, under the discipline of His Word, or to live foolishly. The choice is up to that individual.

With this brief survey complete, the study emphasis now goes to the last chapter of the book and deals specifically with Proverbs 31:10-31. Other passages in Proverbs along with many other portions. of Scripture will also be discussed.

The final chapter of the book of Proverbs contains what is described in the words of King Lemuel, "The prophecy that his mother taught him." According to Dr. H. A. Ironside in his book, *Notes on the Book of Proverbs,* some Bible scholars believe that Lemuel was the "pet" name Bathsheba gave to her son, Solomon. History records no King Lemuel among those who sat on the thrones of either Judah or Israel; nor is there any record of a king by that name among the surrounding nations. It occurs only in this chapter of Proverbs. The word simply means "unto God," or "with God."[4]

It is most interesting and deeply enlightening to be permitted to listen to a part of the instructions given by his mother to the young prince. Assuming this mother is Bathsheba, very little is known about her aside from her seduction by King David. Even that does not indicate her true character. In Proverbs 31, we see grace has dealt with Bathsheba. In light of this, she can be her son's guide and counselor in matters of great importance. No doubt the loss of Bathsheba's firstborn, taken away in the Lord's discipline, made Solomon all the dearer to her heart (2 Sam. 12:24, 25). Solomon probably spent a great deal of time with his mother during his early years, learning to greatly value her instruction and loving care. He was indebted to her for the godliness that marked his early reign. The influence of a God-fearing mother goes beyond all measure (2 Tim. 1:5; 3:15).

The first nine verses of Proverbs 31 are a list of instructions to the young prince, Lemuel, to take heed of the temptations that would face him and instructions to fulfill the duties of the position to which he was called.

The following twenty-two verses are an acrostic poem. Each verse begins with one of the letters of the Hebrew alphabet. This was a favorite form of composition among the Hebrews and is used frequently in the Psalms and in the Lamentations of Jeremiah.

Verses 10 through 31 are the lovely description of a virtuous woman, especially in the capacity of wife and mother of a family. Perhaps Bathsheba drew these up, not in praise of herself (though, no doubt, it was her own true picture), but as instructions to her daughters, as the previous verses were to her son, or as a direction to her son in the choice of a wife: a wife must be chaste and modest, diligent and frugal, dutiful to her husband, careful of her family, discreet in her discourse, and in the education of her children, and above all, conscientious in her duty to God. Such a wife as this would bring a husband much happiness—if he could find her! A virtuous woman is not found by every man; she is found by comparatively few.

The primary purpose of this study is to look at the woman described in Proverbs 31 and to observe her character (her quality, pattern of behavior, moral strength and self-discipline; her distinguishing traits) and to develop these character qualities in our own daily lives.

The picture of this virtuous woman (worthy, noble or excellent as some translations read) is given to women in all stations of life—single, married, or previously married—as a pattern or example of womanhood for today. *Webster's New World Dictionary* defines a pattern as "a person or thing so ideal to be worthy of imitation; a model; guide; sample; definite direction; tendency or characteristic." This pattern is a goal for us to aim toward. As it has been said, "he who aims at nothing will surely hit it"—nothing!

As we proceed through this study, we will be observing other Bible women who are also patterns for us to follow. Let us make our target God's ideal for womanly excellence. With His help, we can achieve our goal.

Begin today to memorize Proverbs 31:10-31 by writing out the verses on four-by-six inch index cards (10-14; 15-19; 20-24; 25-31) and memorize a few at a time until you have completed the entire chapter.

Listed below is the passage from Proverbs 31:10-31 from the *King James Version* of the Bible. Following each verse is the form of the Hebrew letter, the English letter, and the English transliteration so that the acrostic poetry style can be seen.

10. *Who can find a virtuous woman? for her price is far above rubies* (א · A · Aleph).

11. *The heart of her husband doth safely trust in her, so that he shall have no need of spoil* (ב · B · Beth).

12. She will do him good and not evil all the days of her life (ג · C · Gimel).
13. She seeketh wool, and flax, and worketh willingly with her hands (ד · D · Daleth).
14. She is like the merchants' ships; she bringeth her food from afar (ה · E · He).
15. She riseth also while it is yet night, and giveth meat to her household, and a portion to her maidens (ו · F · Vau).
16. She considereth a field, and buyeth it: with the fruit of her hands she planteth a vineyard (ז · G · Zain).
17. She girdeth her loins with strength, and strengtheneth her arms (ח · H · Cheth).
18. She perceiveth that her merchandise is good: her candle goeth not out by night (ט · I · Teth).
19. She layeth her hands to the spindle, and her hands hold the distaff (י · K · Yod).
20. She stretcheth out her hand to the poor; yea, she reacheth forth her hands to the needy (כ · L · Caph).
21. She is not afraid of the snow for her household: for all her household are clothed with scarlet (ל · M · Lamed).
22. She maketh herself coverings of tapestry; her clothing is silk and purple (מ · N · Mem).
23. Her husband is known in the gates, when he sitteth among the elders of the land (נ · O · Nun).
24. She maketh fine linen, and selleth it; and delivereth girdles unto the merchant (ס · P · Samech).
25. Strength and honor are her clothing; and she shall rejoice in time to come (ע · R · Ayin).
26. She openeth her mouth with wisdom; and in her tongue is the law of kindness (פ · S · Pe).
27. She looketh well to the ways of her household, and eateth not the bread of idleness (צ · T · Tsaddi).
28. Her children arise up, and call her blessed; her husband also, and he praiseth her (ק · U · Koph).
29. Many daughters have done virtuously, but thou excellest them all (ר · W · Resh).
30. Favor is deceitful, and beauty is vain: but a woman that

> *feareth the Lord, she shall be praised* (‎ש‎ · Y · Schin).
>
> 31. *Give her of the fruit of her hands; and let her own works praise her in the gates* (‎ת‎ · Z · Tau).[5]

TASKS FROM A to Z

"Man works from sun to sun,
But woman's work is never done."

We have so many hats to wear
It almost drives us to despair.

As we look at our tasks from A to Z
Lord, our strength can only come from Thee.

A - As a creative ARTIST I must see
     That the household decor pleases my family.

B - Being a BOOKKEEPER is not really my bag,
     And often our bank account will sag.

C - They say "a stitch in time saves nine,"
     And as a CLOTHES DESIGNER, I do real fine.

D - "No matter where I serve my guests,
     They seem to like my kitchen best,"
     So being a DIETICIAN is quite a quest.

E - And as an ENTERTAINER I must be,
     Angels might accept my hospitality.

F - As a FARMER I might not have the best crop,
     But it certainly saves on groceries when I shop.

G - Flowers for the GARDENER are so much fun,
     And it's a good excuse to be in the sun.

H - Often to my neighbors a HELPER I can be,
     This is one way, Lord, I can serve Thee.

I · The FBI probably wouldn't want me as an INVESTIGATOR,
But I'll find out who broke that window—sooner or later.

J · JUDGE and JURY I sometimes must be
In order to convict the guilty party.

K · Into the category of KEEPER, many responsibilities fall,
But husband and children are the greatest of all.

L · Wives should always be LOVERS too,
This is a job no one else can do.

M · The MUSICIAN in me may sometimes say,
"I can't stand that trumpet one more day."

N · Fixing skinned knees is my job as a NURSE:
I'm just thankful it wasn't any worse.

O · The telephone can often keep me busy
And acting as OPERATOR puts me in a tizzy.

P · As a PSYCHOLOGIST I don't always understand,
But I'm available to do what I can.

Q · Being the household QUARTERMASTER,
I try to see that my troops don't have a disaster.

R · I sometimes have to REFEREE,
And then they turn on me!

S · But as the SHEPHERDESS of my flock,
My counsel carries a little stock.

T · If my child doesn't heed me as his TEACHER,
I'll take him to see the preacher!

U · To call myself a UROLOGIST is quite a title,
But to a diaper-wet baby, I'm his idol.

V · Preparing clothing for summer, winter, spring and fall,
Keeps this VALET washing and ironing for them all.

W · The tips I receive as a WAITRESS
Often are left in the form of thanks or a caress.

X · It's rather sobering to think
This young child may be a XEROX copy of me—
Printed with indelible ink.

Y · As a YOKEFELLOW to my husband sweet,
We must together guide those little feet.

Z · A ZEALOT I may be when it comes to my family,
But thank you Lord for all these tasks.
Help me to remember,
"Only what's done for Thee will last."

Class Suggestions

Listed below are some suggestions for adding "spice" to the lessons that I have tried with my classes. A 2-2½ hour class time will be necessary for the lesson, discussion and a coffee break, plus a special feature if desired. I usually begin with a brunch or luncheon as a "sign-up/kick off " one week prior to the official beginning of the class.

I trust this study of *Pattern From Proverbs 31* will be helpful and fun as you seek to be the woman God would have you to be. It is a rather flexible study and has been used as a weekly Bible study and also in a two-week vacation Bible school class for women. Thank you for your interest and may God bless you.

Sharon K. Rhoades

Lesson 1—Pattern for Virtuousness

Discuss the use of various Bible commentaries, dictionaries, concordances and translations at the beginning of the class time. Perhaps you could invite the pastor to lead in this discussion. After lesson 1 has been studied, break into groups to begin memorizing Proverbs 31:10-31.

Lesson 2—Pattern for Trustworthiness

Have a craft time after the lesson, such as making silk flowers or macrame.

Lesson 3—Pattern for Energy

Discuss and do exercises as a group or have a style show. Exercise, clothing and makeup are all discussed in lesson 4.

Lesson 4—Pattern for Beauty

This lesson discusses outward and inward beauty and usu-ally takes a full class time. If you would like to have a makeup demonstration by a consultant, stop at page 73, question 8, to allow time for the first half of the lesson and the demonstration; continue question 9 the following week.

Lesson 5—Pattern for Stewardship

Discuss spiritual gifts and help ladies to identify their gifts. The pastor may also want to be in on this discussion after the lesson.

Lesson 6—Pattern for Serving

Assign projects to the gals to help meet some needs in the church. There are some suggestions on page 105. Ask your pastor for ideas.

Lesson 7—Pattern for Preparedness

Invite the home economist from the local extension agency to be the guest speaker to talk about home canning, freezing, etc.

Lesson 8—Pattern for Prudence

I use a tape, "How to Schedule Your Time" by Elaine Colsten, from Christian Womanhood, Box 189, Hammond, IN 46325 (approximately $3.00).

Lesson 9—Pattern for Love

Craft—wheat weaving, calligraphy; write "love notes" for family.

Lesson 10—Pattern for Praise

End with coffee, brunch or lunch and a time of testimony. Encourage the ladies to discuss whether these Bible studies have been helpful.

Prayer Pals

At the close of each lesson, share prayer requests and assign "Prayer Pals" for the week with the reminder to pray each day for the pal.

SAMPLE OF PRAYER PAL REQUESTS

Prayer Pal   Prayer Pal

Date _____   Date _____
Name _____   Name _____

Requests   Requests

	Prayer Pal		Prayer Pal
Date _____		Date _____	
Name _____		Name _____	
	Requests		Requests

Helpful Books

Listed below are some books and booklets that are inexpensive and helpful with this study of Proverbs 31.

Beauty Is Not Enough by Jeanne Hendricks
  (Story of the life of Esther for lesson 7)
  Dallas Theological Seminary
  3909 Swiss Avenue
  Dallas, TX 75204

The Ideal Christian Mother by Theodore Epp
  (A commentary on Proverbs 31)
  Back to the Bible
  Lincoln, NE 68501

Me? Obey Him? by Elizabeth Rice Handford
  (Helpful with lesson 2 regarding submission)
  Sword of the Lord Publishers
  Box 1099
  Murfreesboro,TN 37130

Your Pastor and You by Richard DeHaan
  (Also goes with lesson 2 discussion)
  Radio Bible Class
  Box 22
  Grand Rapids, MI 49555

NOTES

1. Matthew Henry, *Commentary on the Whole Bible* (McLean, VA: Mac-Donald Publishing Co., 1706), 971.

2. Irving J. Jensen, *Proverbs* (Chicago: Moody Bible Institute, 1976), 6.

3. Ibid., 13.

4. H. A. Ironside, *Notes on the Book of Proverbs* (New York: Loizeaux Brothers, 1908), 466, 467.

5. Ibid., 472–485.

Lesson 1

PATTERN FOR VIRTUOUSNESS

Who can find a virtuous woman? for her price is far above rubies (Proverbs 31:10).

Hayil is the Hebrew word for virtuous, denoting strength or ability, often involving moral worth. Sometimes the word is used in its Old English sense of "power" (Mark 5:30; Luke 6:19; 8:46) and "strength" (2 Cor. 12:9). The phrase *"a virtuous woman"* (Ruth 3:11; Prov. 12:4; 31:10, 29), is literally *a woman of ability.*[1]

According to the dictionary, virtue is "general moral excellence; right action and thinking; goodness or morality." Virtuous is "having, or characterized by, moral virtue; righteous; chaste. Having effective virtue or potency."

The virtuous woman is a woman of strength; though the weaker vessel, she is yet made strong by wisdom and grace and fear of God. The same word sometimes translated *strength* is used in the character of good judges in Exodus 18:21.

1. What are the qualities listed in this verse?

_____

_____

A virtuous woman is a woman of spirit; she is in control of her own spirit and is sensitive to other people's spirits; she is pious and industrious and a help meet for man.

Virtuous is also used in the sense of thriftiness and devotion. The thought of chastity is of course included because the devoted wife is faithful to her husband. A virtuous woman is one who is pure, who abstains from a sexual relationship other than with her husband, a woman who is not suggestive; she is free from obscenity and indecency; she is modest, pure and decent.

Many other beneficial qualities are possessed by the virtuous woman. She is a dependable woman and can be counted on in every emergency. She is capable and energetic with a sense of dignity and importance in administering the operations of the home.

This tenth verse of Proverbs 31 seems to indicate that good women are hard to find: *"her price is far above rubies."* This does not refer to buying a wife but to the value of such a woman. Abraham sent his servant to a distant land to search for a bride for his son, Isaac (Gen. 24:3, 4). Perhaps one reason for the rarity of a virtuous woman is that she is seldom sought. **Too often the search is made for accomplishments and external qualities rather than for internal godly worth.** Because virtuous women are rare, they are all the more valued and treasured. Even Adam was not complete until His Creator "made him an help meet for him" (Gen. 2:18).

No man has ever lived who had as much experience with women as King Solomon, who "loved many strange women." He had 700 wives, princesses, and 300 concubines, all of whom it would seem were idolaters. It is easy to understand how they turned Solomon's heart away from God.

2. Read and summarize 1 Kings 11:1-8. _____

_____

_____

_____

The "strange" women Solomon loved were foreign women, or women who were not Israelites. When men of Israel took wives from other lands, they trespassed against the Lord. In Proverbs, however, the strange women Solomon writes about were actually harlots. "The son of a strange woman" in Judges 11:1, 2 is a parallel to the "son of a harlot" (or prostitute). In no other book in the Bible besides Proverbs do we find so many references to loose women and grim warnings against any association with them.

Because of Solomon's gross adultery and idolatry, the kingdom he had raised to majestic heights was tragically torn in two. Solomon's sin destroyed his kingdom. Cleaving to his hundreds of heathen wives (none of whom are named in the Bible except for Naamah, mother of Rehoboam), Solomon could be expected to say something regarding the vices and virtues of women.

3. Summarize Proverbs 5. Describe the characteristics of the prostitute and the results of spending time with one.

_____

_____

_____

4. What is said in the following verses regarding a prostitute?

Proverbs 2:11-16 _____

Proverbs 7:5 _____

Proverbs 23:27 _____

Proverbs 23:28 _____

"Aware that woman was bone of Adam's bone and flesh of his flesh, (Genesis 2:23) Israel's spiritual leaders advocated respect for women and were ready to praise their diligence, piety and qualities, which they valued more highly than their beauty. It is tragic that a notorious polygamist like King Solomon did not illustrate his own proverbs in his life, 'Whoso findeth a wife findeth a good thing, and obtaineth favour of the Lord,' Proverbs 18:22. He would no doubt have been a greater spiritual force if he would have had one prudent wife from the Lord (Proverbs 19:14). Because of his multiplicity of wives, Solomon's reign ended in tragedy and the forfeiture of divine favor."[2]

After discussing vice and virtue, trace with interest Solomon's references to women in Proverbs. Having hundreds of women around him, he learned a great deal about their influence.

5. Read the following verses and describe the   character of

the woman portrayed. Is her pattern of life an influence for good or bad?

Proverbs 5:18 _____

Proverbs 6:24, 25 _____

Proverbs 6:29 _____

Proverbs 7:10-12 _____

Proverbs 9:13 _____

Proverbs 11:16 _____

Proverbs 11:22 _____

Proverbs 12:4 _____

Proverbs 14:1 _____

Proverbs 19:13 _____

Proverbs 21:9, 19 _____

Proverbs 29:3 _____

Proverbs 30:20 _____

Proverbs 30:21, 23 _____

In this women's liberation-crazed twentieth century, when some women are sacrificing their characteristic femininity and nobility and are striving to be more like men, it is encouraging to know that many Christian women—singles, wives and mothers—are striving to keep themselves unspotted from the world and glorifying God by their lives.

When considering the characteristics of a virtuous woman, it is first necessary to understand that a woman cannot reach her goal of excellence without the Lord Jesus Christ and the strength He offers. She must know Christ personally to draw upon this strength. Consider some aspects of getting to know Christ in a personal way in order to become a virtuous woman.

6. What must a woman acknowledge before she can have a personal relationship with Jesus Christ (Rom. 3:23)? _____

_____

7. What is God's remedy for sin (1 Cor. 15:3, 4)? _____

_____

8. On what terms does God make salvation available to the sinner (Rom. 6:23)? _____

9. What is the only way of salvation?

John 1:12 _____

John 3:16 _____

John 14:6 _____

10. When is the best time to consider one's eternal destiny (2 Cor. 6:2)? _____

11. A Christian is one who is trusting in the Lord Jesus for salvation by _____ (Eph. 2:8, 9).

12. What are God's assurances of salvation (John 6:39, 40)?

_____

13. Christians are eternally secure because they are sealed with _____ (Eph. 1:13; Phil. 1:6).

14. On Whom does the Christian depend for enabling power (Acts 1:8)? _____

Becoming a Christian is as easy as A-B-C:

A - Admit your sin   Romans 3:23; Isaiah 53:6
B - Believe Jesus died to pay   Acts 4:12; 16:31; John 3:16;
      sin's penalty   Romans 6:23
C - Call upon the Lord to save   Romans 10:13
      you

If you have never prayed, taking this step of faith by asking Jesus to come into your life to be your Savior and Lord, do it today. Tomorrow may be too late. This personal relationship with Him is a must, not only for daily living, but for eternal life with Jesus in Heaven.

Suggested Prayer:
Dear Father, I admit that I am a sinner and I need Your forgiveness. I believe that Jesus died on the cross for my sin. I now
call upon Jesus to come into my heart and life as my personal
Savior. In Jesus' name. Amen.

Now tell someone you invited the Lord into your heart and
life. Romans 10:10 instructs a new believer, "For with the heart
man believeth unto righteousness; and with the mouth confession
is made unto salvation."

Jesus said in Matthew 10:32 and 33, "Whosoever therefore
shall confess me before men, him will I confess also before my
Father which is in heaven. But whosoever shall deny me before
men, him will I also deny before my Father which is in heaven."

PERSONAL APPLICATION

1. Do not be like King Solomon and let the influence of the world
lead you astray and away from what you know is right according
to God's Word and way.

2. One of woman's greatest assets is her influence. She has a
unique way of leaving the imprint of her character and words upon
every life she touches. She may inspire to great heights or drag
to the lowest scum of earth's society. She is often unaware of the
operation of this powerful tool she possesses. Make sure your
influence on others is positive and honoring to the Lord.

3. Perhaps you know of some sins in your life that are causing
guilt feelings and loss of fellowship with God. Confess these sins
and forsake them. Read 1 John 1:9 and Psalm 51.

4. A virtuous woman is a complete, happy, fulfilled woman when
she has the characteristics of the Proverbs lady. She is the per-
sonification of all the virtues and strengths of character demonstrated throughout the book of Proverbs. She is definitely a pattern
for all to follow.

5. Call daily upon the Holy Spirit's power to help you live a virtuous
life that is pleasing to God and a testimony to others around you.

6. Begin your memorization of Proverbs 31:10-31.

7. Read one chapter of Proverbs a day for the next month.

NOTES

1. James Orr, *International Standard Bible Encyclopedia* (Grand Rapids: Wm. Eerdmans Publishing Co., 1939), 3057.

2. Herbert Lockyer, *All the Women of the Bible* (Grand Rapids: Zondervan Publishing Co., 1967), 270.

Lesson 2

PATTERN FOR TRUSTWORTHINESS

The heart of her husband doth safely trust in her, so that he shall have no need of spoil. She will do him good and not evil all the days of her life (Proverbs 31:11, 12).

The greatest gift of God is a pious, amiable spouse who fears God, loves his house, and with whom one can live in perfect confidence. Martin Luther[1]

"A PIOUS, AMIABLE SPOUSE" means that this woman is God-centered as well as man-centered. A woman who loves God in a righteous way, expressing warmth and true affection, is a desirable wife. This woman will develop the characteristics of love, joy, peace, longsuffering, gentleness, goodness, faith, meekness and temperance as described in Galatians 5:22, 23. Such a woman will automatically be friendly, have a pleasant disposition, be good natured and pleasant to live with—a wife in which the heart of her husband can trust. A woman with these qualities when entering marriage will make it her business to please her husband (1 Cor. 7:34).

The virtuous woman of Proverbs is a woman of spirit herself; yet "her desire is to her husband," to know his mind, that she may accommodate herself to him, and she is willing that "he should rule over her" (Gen. 3:16). She conducts herself in such a way that he has complete confidence in her.

Trusting his wife deals with more than faithfulness in the physical relationship; it is much more encompassing. The husband in Proverbs trusts his wife's chastity of which she never gives him the least occasion to be jealous. Because she is modest and has all the marks of virtue in her countenance and behavior, his *"heart doth safely trust in her."* The Hebrew word for trust, *batach,* means to lean on, trust or be confident. Her husband relies on his wife and takes refuge in her.

She is also scrupulous as she keeps her family's possessions intact. Her husband can leave home for work or on an extended business trip and be completely relaxed. He has absolute confidence in his wife's ability to handle all the things that have to be done with prudence and discretion. She is capable, intelligent and conscientious while handling the "home front" with his best interests in mind. Her husband knows that his return home will be welcomed with a smile. With such a precious jewel as this woman for his wife, the husband has no misgivings. He need not look into the matters entrusted to her with a suspicious eye. He has no reservation or jealousy. He rules in his sphere without and encourages her in her sphere within. A faithful wife and a confiding husband mutually bless each other.

Can the heart of your husband trust you to take disappointment and difficulties, or do you become hysterical, belligerent, argumentative, withdrawn and critical? If your husband were to lose his job, could he trust you to build him up? Would you work hard at stretching the budget? Would you encourage him emotionally, and pray with him and for him about the situation?

Being the woman her husband can trust is one of the jobs of "wifing." It requires constant effort, but it reaps great rewards in appreciation and love.

"She will do him good and not evil all the days of her life." The virtuous woman will comfort her husband, encourage him, be submissive to him, love, honor and obey him all the days of her life, "till death they do part." She is oriented toward her husband; she is not independent and oriented toward herself or solely toward her children. In her concern for her husband, she recognizes her task is to be a help to him—the responsibility of *help meet.* What a woman! It is no wonder her price is far above rubies! No woman intentionally goes into marriage with the idea of doing evil to her husband. It would be completely ridiculous to plan to hinder the one with whom her future is so closely entwined.

Instead of abusing confidence, this trustworthy woman daily seeks to make herself more worthy of her husband's confidence.

She is concerned how she may please her husband—to do him good and not evil. If only this would always be the case. But look at Eve the help meet becoming the tempter (Gen. 3:6); Solomon's wives drawing away his heart (1 Kings 11:1-5); Jezebel stirring up her husband to abominable wickedness (1 Kings 21:25); Job's wife calling upon her husband to "curse God, and die" (Job. 2:9); and the painful cross of "the brawling woman" (Prov. 21:9; 25:24). This is a fearful contrast—evil, not good.[2]

Often there is a mixture of evil with good. Rebekah cared for her husband; yet, in the act of opposition to God, wickedly deceived him (Gen. 27); Rachel loved Jacob, yet brought idolatry into his family (Gen. 31:19; 35:1-4); Michal did good to David at first in preserving his life, evil afterwards in despising him as God's servant (1 Sam. 19:12; 2 Sam. 6:20-22).[3]

The picture of the Proverbs woman is good, not evil. To live for her husband is her highest happiness. This implies subjection but not inferiority. No greater glory could be desired in the husband/wife relationship than that it should illustrate "the great mystery" of Christ and His Church—her trials His and His cause hers.

However, doing her husband good may not come easily. Helping him, supporting him, uplifting him and comforting him are hard work. Perhaps one of the reasons a wife fails to do her husband good is because she is confused about her role. What and who is a wife? What is best for her husband?

Jay Adams in his book, *Christian Living in the Home*, asks two questions: "Husbands, do you love your wives enough to die for them? Wives, do you love your husbands enough to live for them?"[4]

It has been said that dying for a cause is often easier than living for a cause. If this is true, then women may have the harder part of the marriage bargain, for they must do the living for the cause of a happy home and husband.

A wife can contribute so much to her husband's contentment and satisfaction *"that he shall have no need of spoil"* (no temptation to dishonest gain) as she manages his affairs at home. Her husband is not going to have to pick up discarded newspapers or empty aluminum cans on the way home from work to earn the extra money to make ends meet because his wife is squandering away the money; nor does he have to get a part-time job pumping gas to cover the debts caused by his wife.

Read the passage in Ephesians 5:22-33 defining the marriage relationship. In these verses are the keys to marital success. These verses show the lovely picture of the mutual relationship of Christ and the Church: the latter owning Him as Head and delighting to love and serve Him, while Christ finds His joy in the Church and beholds in her an inheritance of untold value. The husband-wife relationship and Christ and the Church are pictured in Ephesians 5:21-25.

To many women, the idea of being submissive sounds degrading. In an era when women have decided not to be content with unequal social and professional status, willingness to be submissive to a husband sounds unfair and old-fashioned. However, this injunction is Scriptural and not to accept this teaching is to disobey the authority of God's Word. There are both practical and theological reasons behind the concept of submission.

Practically, there must be final authority in every organization or there will be anarchy and chaos. Marriage is a cooperative venture, but it is not a democracy or a division between partners.

Theologically (and to Christian women, these reasons should be of prime importance) there are two reasons for the concept of the wife's submission. First, there is creation. God saw fit to create Adam first. Eve came second and she was the help meet (a helper suited or fit for Adam).

Secondly, there is the Fall. First Timothy 2:14 states Eve was deceived, not Adam, when she took of the forbidden fruit. Because of this, Adam was to rule over Eve (Gen. 3:16). The wife is put under the dominion of her husband. "If man had not sinned, he would always have ruled with wisdom and love; and, if the woman had not sinned, she would always have obeyed with humility and meekness. Those wives who not only despise and disobey their husbands, but domineer over them, do not consider that they are under a divine law to be in subjection to their husbands."[5]

Another reason for following the Biblical principles for headship is because it works! When the husband assumes the position of leader as God intended, and the wife has an attitude of submission, marriage will succeed.

To be submissive to her husband does not mean a wife gives up her right to think or to be an individual or becomes less of a person. Ephesians 5 does not say she has to be an emotional dishrag. The Proverbs lady is not.

The key to submission is that the Bible tells a wife to be submissive; therefore, she must do it. Before she is willing to be subject to her husband, she must be willing to be submissive to the Lord. Only when she has a proper relationship with the Lord will she be willing to obey God's Word. When a wife is submissive to the Lord, she can be submissive to her husband.

A wife is doing her husband the greatest good when she allows him to be head of their home. It is not an easy job for him. Again quoting from Jay Adams, "As manager, your husband bears many fearful responsibilities. Perhaps the most perplexing and difficult of all his responsibilities is managing you! Think about it for a while. If you think it's a difficult job to submit, think about his job. He must manage you."[6]

To many women, submission carries threatening overtones. They visualize Jesus as their Shepherd and themselves as sheep under His loving care, and they find it easier to yield to His lordship spiritually than to people in authority over them.

Submission is defined as "yielding, surrendering, giving way to." A natural tendency is to confuse submission with servitude and to picture one who is submissive as downtrodden and abused—a "doormat." Romans 8:6 and 7 explain that natural reasoning is opposite to the purposes and will of God.

Jesus Christ is the Example as in His humanity He set the pattern for perfect submission and total dependence on God.

1. Read Philippians 2:5-11. What choice did Jesus make (vv. 6-8)? _____

_____

_____

2. What was His purpose (Heb. 10:7)? _____

3. Whose will did Jesus consider (John 5:30)? _____

"This is the way the Son obeyed the Father. Submission is an attitude before it is an act. It is an attitude of will that bends eagerly and willingly under the hand of God, seeking ways to obey. There is no stubbornness. It does not consider its own ends and desires because it is lost in the purposes of God. To submit to

God is more than to simply obey. It is to abide in Him, to rest in Him, to lean on Him, to trust Him, to adhere to Him, and to abandon oneself to Him. This is submission—complete confidence that God's plan for us is the very best thing that could happen to us."[7]

When individuals have confessed Christ as Savior, they are individually "in Him" and simultaneously are members of each other; they are "living stones" who make up the Church. Christians are under His authority individually and corporately at the same time. For their protection God has set up this divine order.

4. In what areas of life are we under delegated authority of God?

1 Peter 2:13, 14 _____

Romans 13:1 _____

Ephesians 5:22-24 _____

Daily, in every part of life, Christians come under the influence of God's delegated authorities. In the home God protects by establishing an order created to give perfect unity and strength.

5. What is the order of the home?

1 Corinthians 11:3 _____

Ephesians 6:1 _____

To be subordinate is to be "under the power or authority of another; subservient or submissive" (having or showing a tendency to submit without resistance; yielding).

6. Who is the spiritual head and authority over the Church (Eph. 1:20-23)? _____

7. As a result of the Church's submission to this authority, what will be its ultimate state (Eph. 5:27)? _____

Paul compares marriage to Christ and His relationship with the Church in Ephesians 5:32. Christian marriage is designed to be a reflection of a spiritual truth. The world should be able to see in marriage the love and willing self-sacrifice that characterizes the relationship between Christ and His Church.

A study of history and culture shows that women are constructed to be more physically vulnerable to attack than men. This same vulnerability is also evident in the realm of emotions and spirit; therefore, God places women under the headship of men for their own protection.

God's Order for the Family

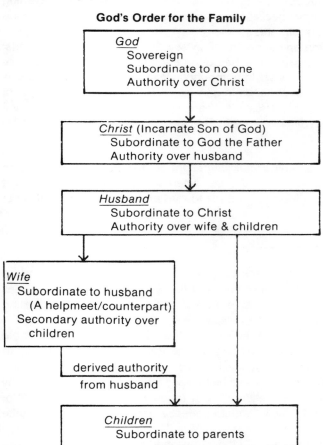

8. What do you think it means to submit yourself to your own husband "as unto the Lord" (Eph. 5:22-33)? _____

_____

If you are an unmarried woman, headship is provided for you through your father. Widowed or divorced women who need help or counseling should consult pastors, deacons and those in the church with delegated spiritual authority. Unmarried women should seek advice from their fathers and church leaders not only for spiritual counseling, but also when problems arise concerning jobs, financial decisions and other matters to which the husband would normally attend.

A woman cannot truthfully say she is yielded to Jesus Christ while at the same time harboring a spirit of rebellion toward those whom God has set in authority as leaders. She may think she is in God's will, engaged in service for Him, but if the principle of rebellion (lawlessness) is operating in her toward authority, she is living in disobedience to God's will (1 Sam. 15:23; Prov. 17:11; 1 John 3:4).

9. In examining your life in light of the verses listed above, do you recognize a specific area where this attitude of rebellion is at work regarding your attitude toward anyone set in authority over you? If so, state it.

Numbers 12 records the account of Miriam and Aaron when they spoke against or criticized the leadership of Moses. Charles Ryrie suggests that the verb 'spoke' is feminine singular, indicating that Miriam led in the criticism."[8]

Matthew Henry comments that "Moses did not resent the injury done him, nor complain to God, nor make any appeal to Him, but God resented it. He hears all we say in our passion, and is a swift witness of our hasty speeches, which is a reason why we should resolutely bridle our tongues, that we speak not ill of others, and why we should patiently stop our ears, and not take notice of it, if others speak ill of us."[9]

In Numbers 12:4 God summoned Miriam, Aaron and Moses to the tabernacle (meeting tent). Moses had often defended God's honor, now God was defending Moses. (Those who honor God, God will also honor; 1 Sam. 2:30.) God asked Miriam and Aaron in verse 8, ". . . were ye not afraid to speak against my servant Moses?" Again quoting from Matthew Henry, " 'How dare you abuse any servant of mine, especially such a servant as Moses, who is a friend, a confident, and a steward of the house.' How dare they speak to the grief and reproach of one whom God had so much to say in commendation of? Might they not expect that God would resent it, and take it as an affront of Himself? We have reason to be afraid of saying or doing any thing against the servants of God; it is our peril if we do, for God will plead their case, and reckon that what touches them touches the apple of His eye. It is a dangerous thing to offend Christ's little ones. Those are presumptuous indeed that 'are not afraid to speak evil of dignities' (2 Pet. 2:10)."[10]

God was so angry with Miriam and Aaron that, according to Numbers 12:10, "The cloud departed from off the tabernacle." This demonstrated God's displeasure. His judgment of Miriam was shown when she became leprous. Leprosy was a disease often inflicted immediately by God as a punishment of sin. "This judgment upon Miriam is improvable by us as a warning to take heed of putting any affront upon our Lord Jesus. If she was thus chastised for speaking against Moses, what will become of those that sin against Christ?"[11]

What were the results of the sin of jealousy that caused Miriam and Aaron to criticize Moses? First, it produced uncleanness as shown by Miriam's leprosy. Faultfinders and backbiters will soon be found outside the service of God. When Christian workers become envious and critical of leadership, trouble is bound to happen. Unfortunately, women are often found at the root of problems within the church, even to the point of causing a church split.

Secondly, this criticism caused interrupted fellowship according to verse 14, ". . . let her be shut out from the camp seven days. . . ." The spirit of jealousy and criticism quickly destroys the spirit of communion and makes a Christian unfit for fellowship with God and fellow believers. This lack of brotherly love grieves the Holy Spirit and the attitude of prayer and worship is lost.

The third aspect of this situation was that progress was hindered (Num. 12:15). The entire camp was kept back because of Miriam's sin. Those who sin in high places of leadership in the church are a great hindrance to the advancement of the cause of Christ. One fly may spoil the ointment, one Achan may cause defeat to the entire army of God, one sin will hinder growth in the

Christian life by marring the testimony and making the life unfruitful. Psalm 139:23 and 24 should be a daily prayer: "Search me, O God, and know my heart: try me, and know my thoughts: And see if there be any wicked way in me, and lead me in the way everlasting."

When recognizing and repenting of rebellion against God-appointed authority, attitudes will change. Submissiveness is not an outward form or a role of foolish servitude; it is an attitude of the heart. It is a willingness to obey God, and in this obedience of yielding self-will to His delegated authority, a woman will know the will of God for her life. The highest respect anyone can give God is to obey Him.

Since everything that comes from God is meant for good, women find that coming into an attitude of submission produces freedom. A train is created to run on a track. As long as the train stays on its track, it is free to fulfill that purpose for which it was made. When it jumps the track, chaos is the result.

The husband's headship and the wife's submission can be likened to a musical duet—both voices must be heard. The husband is responsible for carrying the tune and the wife harmonizes with and supports him. Marriage is God's idea, therefore, His organization. He made the husband to be president and the wife vice-president; both are necessary even though they function differently.

10. According to Romans 13:5, why should we be submissive? _____

_____

God's laws do not change. When people break them, they are in reality only breaking themselves against them. Wives must learn to obey their husbands and to obey other members of the Body of Christ who have authority as God's delegates. In the honoring of and submission to these leaders, women are honoring and being submissive to the Lord (1 Pet. 5:5, 6).

11. What is one purpose for the creation of woman in Genesis 2:18? _____

_____

One commentary explains the Hebrew word for help meet is a "help answering to him, or, one who answers." The Amplified Bible says this help meet is "suitable, adapted, completing" for man.

12. What does *help meet* mean to you? _____

_____

13. According to the following verses, would a woman help or hinder?

Proverbs 18:22 _____

Proverbs 19:14 _____

Proverbs 21:9, 19 _____

Proverbs 27:15, 16 _____

14. What are the results of a woman being a help meet to her husband and "doing him good"?

Ruth 3:11 _____

Proverbs 31:11 _____

Proverbs 31:28 _____

1 Peter 3:1, 2 _____

Listed below are several verses that speak to women. Do not be discouraged if you fall short of fulfilling the requirements. These are goals to aim for and a woman cannot change overnight. However, she can begin immediately to allow the Holy Spirit to control her attitudes, actions and abilities (Rom. 8:5). This is yielding the selfish will to the will of God.

Write in your own words what each verse means to you for the following questions (15-18) regarding instructions to women.

15. Properly adorned:

1 Timothy 2:9 _____

1 Peter 3:3 _____

16. Gentle and quiet spirit:

1 Peter 3:4 _____

Matthew 5:5 _____

Ephesians 4:2 _____

17. Submissive to husband:

1 Peter 3:5 _____

Ephesians 5:22 _____

18. Titus 2:3 tells older women (physically and/or spiritually) to be an example to younger women. What do these instructions mean to you?

   Holy behavior _____

   Not false accusers _____

1 Timothy 3:11 _____

Ephesians 4:29 _____

Proverbs 20:19 _____

James 3:6 _____

2 Corinthians 12:20 _____

Colossians 3:8 _____

Romans 1:28-31 _____

   Not given to much wine _____

Titus 2:3 _____

Ephesians 5:18 _____

Teachers of good things by teaching (encouraging) younger women:

   To be sober _____

   To love their husbands _____

   To love their children _____

   To be discreet _____

To be chaste _____

To be keepers at home _____

To be good _____

To be obedient to their husbands _____

19. Why are the above instructions to be carried out (Titus 2:5)? _____

_____

Women are expected to live in a manner that is above reproach so dishonor and criticism will not be brought on the Word of God.

20. What do Titus 2:7 and 8 admonish? _____

_____

A woman is placed lovingly and carefully by God the Creator in a particular place in His divine plan. There are vast opportunities for service and creativity in her God-ordained role (Titus 2:4, 5). She can rest knowing she is in His perfect will. But when she steps into the role-reversal so common in society today, she is in disharmony with herself, with her family and in her relationship to God (Rom. 13:2).

Dependability and trustworthiness are almost lost arts for many people. However, when one is loyal to Christ in daily living and obedient through submission to those in authority, no one will suffer because of a lack of faithfulness. Jesus said in Revelation 2:10, "Be thou faithful unto death, and I will give thee a crown of life."

PERSONAL APPLICATION

1. If submission "rubs you the wrong way," ask God to change your attitude to "I delight to do thy will" (Ps. 40:8).
2. Pray daily for those in authority over you (your father, husband, pastor, government officials), asking God to give these leaders His wisdom and guidance.
3. Suggested reading: *Me, Obey Him?* Elizabeth Rice Handford;

Let Me Be a Woman, Elisabeth Elliot; *I Am A Woman By God's Design,* Beverly LaHaye; *The Role of Women in the Church,* Charles Ryrie.

4. The definitions of two words frequently used in this study are listed below. It will be helpful to keep these definitions in mind. Write out the accompanying Scripture.

attitude—a bodily posture showing a mental state or mood; manner that shows one's disposition (one's nature or temperament).

One of the greatest, most important attributes you will ever attain is a consistent, even-tempered, controlled, sweet, loving, friendly attitude.

Write out Philippians 2:5. _____

_____

A Christian should voluntarily set aside self-interest and do what is best for others. He should willingly sacrifice and follow God's divine will in putting others' interests ahead of his own. Practicing the mind of Christ will create a climate of peace and good will. The Amplified Bible renders this verse, "Let this same attitude and purpose and [humble] mind be in you which was in Christ Jesus.—Let Him be your example in humility."

In our desire to be like Christ, we display a submissive attitude toward the will of God, making it our highest priority. Our prayer should be as His, "Not my will, but thine, be done." Doing the will of God with a glad heart, we find no reason to gripe or complain against God or others, and we refuse to debate God over the things He brings into our lives. We may not always understand why God deals with us in certain ways, but Romans 8:28 tells us all things work together for our good.

yield—surrender; to concede; grant; to give place. The Greek implies yielding is an act of the will.

The act of the will is demonstrated when a follower is obedient to a leader: wives are to submit to husbands; children are to obey parents; employees are to serve their employer; a citizen is to obey the government; a church is supposed to follow the pastor. A Christian must yield to the Holy Spirit. The weaker is to be in obedience to the stronger.

5. Make a list of all the relationships you have where you are responsible to authority, and if you will decide that you are going to yield yourself to that authority, you will be happy. As the submissive person, it is the responsibility of loyalty to see to it that the one in authority over you succeeds in that leadership position.

---

6. Memorize Psalm 51:10.

7. The following article written by Herbert Vander Lugt (Radio Bible Class) is an aid in "How to Help Your Pastor."

"Every year hundreds of pastors leave the ministry and enter other vocations because they can't handle the difficulties and discouragements of their calling. And many who faithfully continue sometimes have serious bouts with depression. One key factor in this trend is that the pastor's effectiveness is directly dependent upon the voluntary love-motivated service of church members. If you are a Christian, therefore, you ought to ask yourself what you can do to help your pastor fulfill his God-ordained task. You can begin with these:

PRAY—Pray for your pastor and his family. Every sincere minister can identify with the appeal of Paul, 'Now I beseech you, brethren, . . . that ye strive together with me in your prayers to God for me' (Romans 15:30). Your pastor and his family are mere human beings, just like you are. They have the same weaknesses and problems in addition to the special difficulties associated with the public ministry. Therefore, pray for them individually and specifically every day.

SUBMIT—Acknowledge your pastor as the spiritual leader of the congregation. Put into practice the admonition of Hebrews 13:17, 'Obey them that have the rule over you, and submit yourselves: for they watch for your souls, as they that must give account, that they may do it with joy, and not with grief.' True, pastors are not to act as 'lords over God's heritage' (1 Peter 5:3), nor are they to be viewed as infallible dictators. But they do 'have the rule over you,' and every church member should acknowledge their position and calling.

GET BUSY—Third, choose a task in your church and do it energetically and thoroughly. Ask the Lord to direct you. Then take to heart the words of Paul, 'And whatsoever ye do, do it heartily, as to the Lord, and not unto men' (Colossians 3:23). If every ablebodied church member would do one thing well, our pastors would find great joy in their work.

BE HONEST—Fourth, be open and aboveboard with your pastor. If you feel that his ministry is effective, encourage him by telling him so. But if you are convinced that he isn't preaching the whole counsel of God, discuss that with him too. If you know of individuals he is neglecting, tell him in a kind Christian spirit. But please don't spread discord and dissension through the church.

BE PATIENT—Finally, be patient with your pastor. He is an imperfect man working with a group of imperfect people. IN FACT, YOU MAY BE ONE OF HIS HANDICAPS.

In conclusion, your pastor doesn't need sympathy; he needs support. You can help him by praying for him, acknowledging his leadership, taking your responsibilities seriously, and being honest with him."[12]

NOTES

1. Gayle G. Roper, *Wife, Mate, Mother, Me!* (Grand Rapids: Baker Book House, 1975), 18.

2. Charles Bridges, *The Commentary on Proverbs* (Carlisle, PA: The Banner of Truth Trust, 1846), 621.

3. Ibid.

4. Roper, 23.

5. Henry, *Commentary on the Whole Bible,* 31.

6. Roper, 24.

7. Shirley Rice, *The Christian Home* (Norfolk: Norfolk Christian Schools, 1965), 31.

8. Charles Caldwell Ryrie, *The Ryrie Study Bible* (Chicago: Moody Press, 1976), 227.

9. Henry, 614.

10. Ibid., 615.

11. Ibid., 616.

12. Herbert Vander Lugt, "How to Help Your Pastor," *RBC Discovery Digest* (Grand Rapids: Radio Bible Class, 1981), 22. Used by permission.

Lesson 3

PATTERN FOR ENERGY

She seeketh wool, and flax, and worketh willingly with her hands. She is like the merchants' ships; she bringeth her food from afar. She riseth also while it is yet night, and giveth meat to her household, and a portion to her maidens. She considereth a field, and buyeth it: with the fruit of her hands she planteth a vineyard. She layeth her hands to the spindle, and her hands hold the distaff. She maketh fine linen, and selleth it; and delivereth girdles unto the merchant" (Proverbs 31:13-16, 19, 24).

KITTO SAID, "In the state of society to which this description belongs, every kind of drapery for their person, the tent, or the house, is manufactured at home by the women, who make it a matter of pride to be able to boast that their husbands and children are entirely clad by the labor of their hands; and the man's robe clings the more sweetly to him—is warmer in winter, and cooler in the heat, from his knowledge of the dear hands by which every thread has been prepared."[1]

This Proverbs woman is pictured according to the life of ancient times; however, the general principles have universal application for today. It describes a woman who is not only the wife of a man of rank but a wise, useful and godly matron in her domestic responsibilities. It is a woman professing godliness, adorned "with good works" (1 Tim. 2:10); a Mary-Martha woman. One half of this picture of the virtuous woman is occupied with her personal and domestic industry.

In these six verses from Proverbs 31 it is obvious that this lady is a worker—not a shirker. She is never lazy. Her heart, head, hands and feet—in fact, her entire being—is dedicated to the welfare of her household. She finds her deepest joy in loving service; the principle of self-denial is demonstrated here.

This virtuous woman applies herself to the business that is proper for her—not scholar's business, nor statesman's business nor husbandman's business but woman's business as verse 13 states, *"She seeketh wool, and flax."* The Hebrew word for seeketh, *darash,* means to actively pursue or search. This woman does not just settle for whatever the local department store has in stock; she searches diligently for exactly what she needs in the terms of quality, color and price. She is not lazy; she goes after what she needs. If one place does not have it, she goes to another. She has on hand everything that is necessary to carry on both the woolen and linen manufacture.

"She . . . worketh willingly (Hebrew *chehfets) with her hands"* means she works with the counsel or delight of her hands; she goes about it cheerfully, not only with her hands but her mind, and goes on in it without weariness. She sets the pattern of working willingly with her hands—even though spinning flax probably does not win any rewards for mental stimulation. Working willingly is a mental attitude. It is being pleased with housework, having a desire to do it and taking delight in doing it—all for the purpose of glorifying God! So often it is the same old story about dirty dishes. Dirty dishes at breakfast, lunch and dinner—wash them, dirty them, wash them, dirty them—day after day. (The same goes for the laundry and cleaning.) With the affluence in the United States, homemakers should thank God each day for food to dirty the dishes, clothes to wash and a home to keep clean.

No one expects a woman to like everything she has to do—dusting, ironing, washing dishes, matching socks or typing endless letters. However, God does expect Christian women to do these things willingly as unto Him.

1. Write out Ecclesiastes 9:10a. _____

_____

2. Also Colossians 3:17. _____

_____

"Willingly" means she shops wisely; she plans her menus—

vegetables, meat, fruit and milk. She shops at the wholesale out-
lets, saves fortunes on the family clothing because she sews, therefore not getting her husband into debt by overspending. She
passes on to others the clothes the children have outgrown. This
does not mean she has to be a home economist—she just uses
well her basic knowledge and the common sense she has diligently acquired.

3. How can you stretch the family budget with the high prices
of

groceries? _____

clothing? _____

furniture? _____

This virtuous lady is not content with slip-shod service but is
constantly bringing treasures from distant lands with her enter-
prising spirit. No merchant's ship, not even Solomon's navy, ever
made a more advantageous return than her efforts do. She brings
from a distance what is necessary to supply her house. She does
the same with the fruit of her labors. What she produces in her
garden, she can exchange for imported goods and therefore, *"She
is like the merchants' ships; she bringeth her food from afar"*
(v. 14).

Slothfulness she shuns, for verse 15 tells us, *"She riseth also
while it is yet night, and giveth meat to her household, and
a portion to her maidens."* She provides food for her whole household, then she gives the portion of work to her maidens (not the
men servants; these she leaves to her husband).

This Proverbs lady goes before her maidens in diligence, im-
posing nothing upon them that she has not first done herself. She
understands the exact work of each maiden under her care and
their different abilities, when they need to be directed and when
they may be left to their own responsibility.

A woman may say, "Aha! No wonder this Proverbs gal can
whistle while she works; she has at least two maids. If I had maids,
I would be more than happy and willing to be in charge of the
'domestic engineering department' of the household." Women
today may not have maids to help with the housework, but they
do have "maidens" the Proverbs lady certainly does not have. It

has been said, "There's a switch for everything in the home but the children." Today's "household maidens" do not even talk back.

4. List at least ten electrical "maidens" you use in a week's time:

_____

_____

_____

Rising early seems to be a Biblical trait. Dr. Ironside tells us, "In Syria, the women are up long before the dawn to prepare the morning meal, 'grinding at the mill', according to the Lord's description, in order that the men may go forth early to labor, and thus be enabled to rest during the sultry part of the day."[2]

5. The Bible tells us of other people who were early risers. Who are they?

_____ rose early to stand before the Lord (Gen. 19:27).

_____ rose early to worship the Lord (Gen. 28:18).

_____ rose early to give God's message to Pharaoh (Exod. 8:20).

_____ rose early to build an altar to God (Exod. 24:4).

_____ rose early to lead Israel over Jordan (Josh. 3:1).

_____ rose early to capture Jericho (Josh. 6:12).

_____ rose early to examine the fleece (Judg. 6:36-38).

_____ rose early to worship God (1 Sam. 1:9).

_____ rose early to meet Saul (1 Sam. 15:12).

_____ rose early to do as his father asked him (1 Sam. 17:20).

_____ rose early to offer sacrifices for his children (Job 1:5).

_____ rose early to care for her household (Prov. 31:15).

_____ rose early to go to a solitary place to pray (Mark 1:35).

_____ rose early to go to the sepulchre (Mark 16:1, 2).

_____ rose early to go hear Jesus (Luke 21:38).

_____ rose early to go to the temple (John 8:1, 2).

For some, there is nothing harder to take than an early riser who delights in getting up with the sun. Inevitably these people awake singing "Heavenly Sunshine" while in the shower, then eat big breakfasts. They are even ready for their morning appointments early, arriving bright-eyed and bushy-tailed, while the rest of the world looks at them through eyes still unfocused.

The almost universal desire to sleep in is a sneaky trap to which a housewife is especially susceptible. At first, she grabs just a few more minutes, then a few more, until getting up to fix breakfast is just too much. The kids and husband are big enough to fix their own Wheaties. Before she knows it, everyone in the household is gone before she gets up.

The energetic woman loves her household better than her ease or pleasure. She is on duty twenty-four hours a day and has true satisfaction in having *"given meat to her household."* Someone has said, "Those who have a family to take care of should not love their bed too well in the morning." Women cannot stay up and watch the late show and the late-late show and sleep until noon if they expect to get anything accomplished during the day. It is difficult to hoot with the owls at night and expect to soar with the eagles in the morning!

It is very important for a mother to share herself with her family at breakfast. She may not be cheery and chatty, but she can be there. Sending the kids off to school with a smile is an expression of love. A husband needs his send-off too. Do not just let him disappear; that is a sign of apathy. A song that was popular several years ago warned that "Wives Should Always be Lovers, Too." One phrase is, "Don't send him off with your hair still in curlers, you may not see him again." If a wife is still in her housecoat when she sees her husband off to work in the morning, the scene should not be like the cartoons, with her housecoat falling apart and dirty. She should have on a pretty, feminine one with her hair combed and perhaps even a touch of makeup. Another phrase of the song is, "Day after day there are girls in the office, and men will always be men." A wife does not want her husband's secretary to look prettier and smell sweeter than she does first thing in the morning!

Unless ill health dictates a longer than usual rest, most women who sleep in do it for one of two reasons: laziness or boredom.

Laziness is not a problem for the Proverbs lady. She is the picture of busyness and good sense. This does not mean she is not tempted to give up occasionally or that she does not feel like pulling the wool she is spinning. However, it does mean she is mature enough not to give in.

The companion of laziness is boredom, a real problem for many women. Often the most discontented people are women graduates of liberal arts colleges who have to stay home with small children. As each new day dawns, the same old routine confronts them—blow noses, make beds, do dishes, change diapers, wash and clean. They did all that yesterday, so why bother to get up today?

If this is the sum total of your life and the extent of your existence, it is time for a change! Do some searching by prayer and find your answer. Remember the promise in John 10:10. **The abundant life is not some magical state of mind, it is a life centered in Christ-oriented action.** Satan can achieve victory if he keeps women bored and listless. Women with purpose and Christ-centered goals are a powerful force. They are alive, vital and far from being bored.

Here are some suggestions to cure boredom:

1. Ask some of your neighbors (Christian and non-Christian) over one day a week, or every other week, to study the Bible. Or perhaps you could be a babysitter for someone else's Bible study.

2. Join some civic organization whose purpose you support. Go to the YWCA for exercise classes. Volunteer for the PTA board. One sure cure for boredom is to be involved in sharing Christ with others as you get to know them. Take a craft class; learn calligraphy.

3. How about taking a correspondence course from a Bible college or attending your local community college? Do volunteer work at your church by visiting the shut-ins or those in nursing homes, taking your children with you at times. Little people are like sunbeams on a cloudy day to older people.

Each new day, take time to praise God when you first awake. Thank Him for the blessings and challenges the day will bring. "Thank you, Lord, for another morning. Thank you for today. Help me to use it wisely."

Proverbs 31:16 reads, *"She considereth a field, and buyeth it: with the fruit of her hands she planteth a vineyard."* The Hebrew word for considereth, *zamam,* means to plan. The Proverbs lady plans or considers what an advantage the land will be. Perhaps this family lives in the city (v. 23); therefore, it is necessary to purchase a plot of ground in the country in which to plant a garden. This is not done necessarily for the purpose of buying and selling for a profit or to increase the estate, because that would be a business transaction in the husband's realm. However, unlike the unfaithful servant who wrapped his talent in a napkin and hid it away where he could not use it, this lady, by her economy and foresight, adds to her husband's possessions.

Remember the husband in Proverbs 31:11 has complete confidence in his wife so she is free to purchase the land. She does not go into it blindly and take chances. In her consideration of the purchase, she thinks of the advantage the land will be for her entire family. Now she puts the land to use by planting a vineyard or garden. It takes time, money and energy to plant a garden and she does it with the money earned from the merchandise she has produced (v. 18).

Notice, she considers the field first; she is not an impulse buyer. She considers if she can afford to take so much money out of savings to purchase the land; whether the title is good; whether the ground has good soil and will grow a good garden. Today many women pull their husbands under financially because they do not stop to consider all the facts involved before making purchases.

You might be saying this woman is hyper with all the energy she has to do these many things. She is not, but she is not idle either. She carefully plans each day to maximize the utilization of all her resources. In verse 11 the reason why her husband *"has no need of spoil"* or lack of gain is because his wife adds to his worth.

"She layeth her hands to the spindle, and her hands hold the distaff," according to verse 19. This verse has reference to the ancient custom, which is still prevalent among some Eastern people, of spinning without the use of a wheel. This spinning is the tedious process of making thread from the fibers of plants or animals. The woman holds the distaff in one hand and twirls the long wool spindles with the other hand, stopping to wind the thread on them as fast as it is drawn out. The process begins with the

fibers being wrapped around the distaff. The fibers are pulled off
the distaff a few at a time. They move through the woman's fingers
where they are rolled into one continuous thread. Finally, the
thread is wound on the turning spindle, a smooth stick which is
rotated by rolling it against the hip. Slowly the spindle is filled with
thread. Eventually there is enough to weave a piece of material
from which a garment can be cut.[3] It takes a lot of commitment
to do this in order to keep the family in clothing and it is a huge
undertaking for any woman.

Even though a woman does not have to do spinning today,
there are many other time-consuming, energy-draining jobs. In this
category are teaching and training children in the ways of the Lord.
She can put a great deal of time and energy into the church, working with various programs. Friendships also take time to nurture.
However, the most demanding, with the greatest rewards, is that
of working on her marriage. Parents have their children about
twenty years, then they are gone to face the world themselves.
Others help share the work of Christ in the church. Friends are
wonderful, but women do not usually live with them. Marriage is
"till death us do part" and is a life-long project that requires and
deserves prime time and effort.

Moving on to the last verse for consideration in this lesson,
verse 24 says, *"She maketh fine linen, and selleth it; and delivereth girdles unto the merchant."* As has been noted, the lady
in Proverbs is a working mother. She diligently seeks for quality
items for her home, she works willingly and cheerfully in her
domestic duties, she gets up early to see that her household is
run efficiently, she purchases and plants a garden; now she is
dealing with merchants. Not only does she have sufficient items
to clothe her household, but she is able to sell her production of
linen garments and girdles to the caravan merchants who readily
purchase her work to carry to distant lands. Therefore, she is
"bearing fruit in good works" and her abundant labors provide
clothing for those in far-off places. According to Dr. Ironside, "The
spiritual lesson is this—she who is faithful in ministering at home
and clothes herself in a garment of practical godliness and
righteousness, will have enough to spare for the blessing of others
in the regions beyond."[4]

What about the working mother? Today women are achieving

in the business world as never before. There are women doctors, women lawyers and women politicians, mail persons, salespersons and telephone line persons. Many homemakers are being pressured into the thought, "Should I get a job in the business world?" After all, the Bible does not say, "A woman shall not work outside the home."

Read Genesis 1:26-28. Notice the word *them*. Eve worked side by side with Adam as his help meet. Note the working woman in Ruth 2:2, 3. Ruth, the Gentile from whose line the Lord descended, is the central character in this book of the Old Testament. As a widow, she is a working woman and does the job of gleaning. She is not paid a salary, but she earns a living. It is through this work that she meets and marries her employer, Boaz.

6. Who is the working woman in Acts 16:14, 15? What is her occupation?

7. Who is the working couple in Acts 18:1-3? What is their occupation?

For a single girl there is one condition placed on her—she must seek out and do the work that God has for her and she must do her best. All employed persons are admonished to serve their employers well in Ephesians 6:5, 6. However, a married woman must consider, "Wives submit yourselves unto your own husbands" (Eph. 5:22). Here, two lives must be considered. The church should not make decisions without consulting the Lord; therefore, the wife should not make a decision without consulting her husband. If a married woman chooses to work outside the home, it must be with the consent of her husband.

As mentioned before, there are no specific instructions in the Bible regarding women employed outside the home. But before rushing out and getting a job, first consider some Scriptural principles. (Remember Titus 2.)

In Genesis at the time of the Fall, God placed a curse on Adam: "Cursed is the ground for thy sake; in sorrow shalt thou eat of it all the days of thy life. . . . In the sweat of thy face shalt thou eat bread, til thou return unto the ground . . ." (Gen. 3:17, 19).

The first principle here is that man is to labor by the sweat of his brow to feed his family and himself. Therefore, the man feeds the family while the wife cares for the home and children. If "man goeth forth to his work and to his labor until the evening" (Ps. 104:23), then the woman finds her work as a "keeper at home" (Titus 2:5) as she "guides the house" (1 Tim. 5:14). Whose responsibility is it to train the children in the home?

The second principle is that it is the mutual responsibility of both parents to train the children. The man, as head of the family, is to assure that the first principle is fulfilled, but the training of the children is a joint responsibility.

8. What advice is given in the following verses?

Proverbs 29:15 _____

Isaiah 38:19 _____

Isaiah 66:13 _____

Proverbs 3:12 _____

Proverbs 1:8 _____

Deuteronomy 5:16 _____

Traditionally, men have been away from home much of the day "working by the sweat of their brow," while much of the joy and responsibility of the training of the children has fallen to the mother. For many women this pattern is fine today. For other women, with different personalities and desires, the prospect of staying home with little Junior is like a prison. Not that she has anything against Junior, but her education, training and personal desire have created a need for more than this. However, if a mother works full time outside the home, what happens to Junior? Who is responsible for him? If he goes to the babysitter, she must be the type of woman capable of training him because she is assuming the mother's God-given responsibilities while the mother is working.

The November 1978 publication of *The Church Around the World* reported that "41 percent of United States mothers with children under age 6 work outside the home—affecting more than six million children. At least two million children between the ages of 3 and 13 must care for themselves while their mothers work, and 200,000 of the two million are between the ages of 3 and 6."[5] The United States Census Bureau indicated that in 1983 there were 48,503 women working outside the home.[6]

The key consideration for a working woman is whether her job helps or hinders her family. If she has preschoolers, they need mommy around. They need that security moment by moment. A psychologist who works with emotionally disturbed children says the child needs someone "to fuse" with—a "sameone" person—at least for the first three years. He needs a primary model, needs someone to stick around—to be there, someone who is interested, who listens and cares.[7]

A mother with preschoolers should not work outside the home unless there is a dire financial need; that is, her husband is ill, disabled, permanently laid off or deceased. Some mothers with preschoolers have found ways to earn a living at home by babysitting, typing, sewing, baking, proofreading, piano lessons, etc. Many women who go outside the home to find employment are actually making a choice between their families and their finances. The hidden persuader here is insecurity. One of the faults of average Christians is that they get their eyes off the Lord and on the world. Some women are swept off their feet by the swift current of the world; they have earnings rather than eternity in mind.

Even though the apron strings have been cut to some extent, children in school still need assurance and security that only a parent can provide. They need to be able to come home to someone who is patient and loving and just as excited to hear, as they are to tell, all the new things they learned in school.

It is difficult for a working mother to give her job all it requires when she may have left the children crying at the babysitter's at 7:30 in the morning, after having awakened them at 6:00 to get to the sitter's, and then tried to get to work on time. If the sitter comes to the home, it is frustrating if she is the type who eats everything in the refrigerator, watches television all day and does not really pay any attention to the children. Fortunately, not all babysitters are this way.

Consider how an employer feels when the secretary has to leave work in the middle of the day because her child is ill at the sitter's or at school. With two or more young children this can happen often and therefore cuts down on a woman's efficiency on her job. It is always frustrating to other coworkers who have to "cover" for her.

Another factor regarding the working woman is that an unhealthy relationship can develop with other men on the job. She puts her best efforts into the eight to five job to please the boss—who may seem more pleased with her work at the office than her husband and children are with her work at home. Thus she may feel more appreciated at the office than at home. She may become a "listening ear" for her employer because she "understands" him and his wife does not. The two of them become more free in sharing their private lives and soon an employer-employee (or fellow worker) relationship has developed into an affair.

One of the most difficult things for a working mother is the constant emotional and physical stress under which she must live. One woman said, "What bothers me is that I always give my best hours, my best disposition, to someone other than my husband and my children. They always see me at my worst. I go to work feeling fine. By the time I get home, I'm like a dishrag, and I'm afraid I'm as cranky as a bear. If I didn't have to go to work every day, I could be giving my best to the ones I love the most." How can the family feel relaxed around a mother who is tired and irritable?

Sometimes a working woman can be a threat to her husband's self-confidence if she makes more money that he does and if she has a more prestigious position. This can often cause friction in their home.

Another disadvantage to the working woman is that her spiritual life can become anemic. Each morning, a host of Christian women across the country get up by the alarm, gulp down a hurried breakfast (or no breakfast at all), then dash to the office. The majority of these work at secular jobs, year after year. With such a hectic pace of trying to keep house with one hand and with the other hand be efficient on a job, these women have almost no time for the Lord, the One who gave His life for them. They have little time to read and meditate on God's Word and thus are starved spiritually. When these same women go home to be with the Lord, they will practically be strangers to their own Savior, and they will wish they had spent more time serving Him on earth.

Recent research is showing that there is another price women are paying for their venture into what has traditionally been a man's world. That is, women are beginning to fall prey to the same stresses that trigger heart attacks in men, making this a major killer.

Some ladies work because they really do need the money for the family; others work because there is not enough to do at home (perhaps there are no children or maybe the children are older or even grown and gone). Others work because they have abilities that need to be used.

Those wives and mothers who do work outside the home need to be careful that they schedule their time so they can do their work well on the job; be loving, gracious wives to their husbands; train their children in the nurture and admonition of the Lord; keep an attractively clean house; serve the Lord faithfully in all areas of Christian responsibility; and in general be all God wants them to be. This is a big order, but a woman has an all-sufficient Heavenly Father Who does promise to provide her needs and does enable her to do what she should do.

"Do well what you're doing, and do it with all your heart and mind." Many women who work outside the home have learned to do just this. However, other women who remain at home have not learned to give themselves to the enjoyments and responsibilities of each hour. Consequently, it is not always the job outside the home that hinders successful family relationships.

This applies to the time spent with children. Often a mother who is home all day with her children will not take the time to develop a close relationship with her teenage daughter, or get on the floor and play an exciting game with a child, or read a Bible story. Sometimes the quality of time rather than the quantity of time counts the most to a child.

If you and your husband feel it is necessary for you to be a financial help meet (not for *wants* but *needs*) perhaps you should secure part-time work a few hours a day or a couple of days a week. Try to find a job that will correspond with your children's school hours or with your husband's job so that you are working while your husband is home with the children.

If you are contemplating full-time employment, consider the

pros and cons of each of the following and what will be the results. (Copy the chart onto a separate sheet of paper, enlarging the chart about 1½ times.)

CONSIDERATION	PROS	CONS	RESULTS
Husband Family Relationship Self Housework Finances (income versus expense) Other			

Can a woman be a wife, mother, homemaker and employee and not pay for it emotionally, physically and spiritually? What is the value of being a working mother if her children never call her blessed? Is it worth the price to pay if she achieves in the business world and her husband leaves her for another woman?

The Bible does present Christian women with priorities and the responsibility to keep them straight. The order is God, husband, children, home, then outside activities. If women can keep everything properly organized, they will save themselves and their families many heartaches and problems.

The Proverbs lady is a working wife and mother, but she works through her *home.* No doubt some of her creativity requires help from her children—gardening, sewing, cleaning, shopping. Through her creativity and soliciting the children's help, she is also training her children in the "how tos" of these various aspects of homemaking, and in turn teaching them responsibility and preparing them for their future roles. By her industry and self-denial she "buildeth her house" (Prov. 14:1).

The issue of the working mother is difficult. Each woman and her family must face it alone. Circumstances, personalities and compulsions must be prayerfully considered. God has a perfect plan for each woman who seeks it.

9. Write out Psalm 32:8. _____

PERSONAL APPLICATION

1. As a homemaker, "whatsoever thy hand findeth to do" may seem never ending; however, words and deeds are to be done "in the name of the Lord, giving thanks to God."

2. If you feel "trapped" or bored as a homemaker, try a suggestion on page 52.

3. As noted in the lesson, single women are better able to work full time, but a married woman must consider her motive for working: is she discontented with the feminine role? Does she want to use an education, to feel fulfilled, to escape from home, to work solely for materialism?

4. A working woman must be organized to make every minute of the day count. Doing several jobs at once is helpful: while washing the laundry, stick a cake in the oven, then vacuum; fold the laundry as it comes out of the dryer; while on the phone (be sure to get a long phone cord), straighten a room or drawer or do your nails. Get the children to help by training them to pick up after themselves, to dust, to empty waste baskets, to do dishes, to clean their rooms, etc. Planning your menus in a book and shopping from a list will also be helpful.

5. Ask the Lord to guide you daily whether you are at home or at the office, that you will do your jobs willingly and cheerfully, as unto the Lord.

6. List all your responsibilities in the "Domestic Engineering Department" and when your list is completed, there will be no time for boredom!

From My Cupboard Door

THE TEACHER

Lord, who am I to teach the way
To little children day by day,
So prone myself to go astray?
I teach them knowledge, but I know
How faint the flicker and how low
The candles of my knowledge glow.
I teach them power to will and do,
But only now to learn anew
My own great weakness through and
through.
I teach them love for all mankind
And all God's creatures, but I find
My love comes lagging far behind.
Lord, if their guide I still must be
Oh, let the little children see
The teacher leaning hard on Thee.

(From *Some One Special* by Gladys Seashore)

TWO PRAYERS

Last night my little boy
Confessed to me
Some childish wrong;
And kneeling at my knee,
He prayed with tears—
"Dear God, make me a man
Like Daddy—wise and strong;
I know you can."
Then while he slept
I knelt beside his bed
Confessed my sins,
And prayed with low-bowed head,
"O God, make me a child
Like my child here—
Pure, guileless,
Trusting Thee with faith sincere."

Andrew Gillies

A MOTHER'S BEATITUDE

Blessed is the mother who understands her child,
    for she shall inherit a kingdom of memories.
Blessed is the mother who knows how to comfort,
    for she shall possess a child's devotion.
Blessed is the mother who guides by the path of righteousness,
    for she shall be proud of her offspring.
Blessed is the mother who is never shocked,
    for she shall receive confidences.
Blessed is the mother who teaches respect,
    for she shall be respected.
Blessed is the mother who emphasizes the good and minimizes the bad,
    for in like manner the child shall make evaluations.
Blessed is the mother who treats her child as she would be treated,
    for her home shall be filled with happiness.
Blessed is the mother who answers simply the startling questions,
    for she shall always be trusted.
Blessed is the mother who has character strong enough to withstand the
   thoughtless remarks and resentments of the growing child,
    for again, in due time, she shall be honored.

Lenora Zearfoss

NOTES

1. Ironside, *Notes on the Book of Proverbs,* 473, 474.

2. Ibid.

3. Roper, *Wife, Mate, Mother, Me!* 50.

4. Ironside, 480.

5. *Church Around the World* (Wheaton, IL: Tyndale House Publishers, November, 1978).

6. Bureau of the Census, *Statistical Abstract of the United States, 1983* (1984).

7. Ella May Miller, "Problems Working Mothers Face " (Harrisonburg, VA: Heart to Heart, No. 954), n.d.

Lesson 4

PATTERN FOR BEAUTY

She girdeth her loins with strength, and strengtheneth her arms. Her husband is known in the gates, when he sitteth among the elders of the land. Strength and honor are her clothing; and she shall rejoice in time to come (Proverbs 31:17, 23, 25).

WOMEN TODAY NEED TO pattern their lives after this virtuous woman as they gird themselves with strength by directing their minds in a straight and steady course toward things that will give health and peace of mind. God's ideal woman is free from all habits that would injure her physically, mentally or spiritually. She conducts herself in such a manner that she will have nothing of which to be ashamed. She realizes that her body is the temple of the Holy Spirit and she does her best to make it a fit dwelling place for Him.

Verse 17 tells us, *"She girdeth her loins with strength, and strengtheneth her arms."* The Hebrew word *chagar,* for girdeth, literally means to put on as a belt or armor, to encircle or surround. This belt was worn over loose clothing to hold it in place. The loins are the mid-section above the hip bone and below the ribs. The Proverbs woman puts her whole soul into her work as she girds her loins with strength—she is ready to do any work suitable to her. She realizes she must be healthy in order to perform all the strenuous duties she does efficiently. Therefore, she watches her diet and gets plenty of good exercise.

Because there is no European Health Spa close by where this lady can work out, she strengthens herself naturally. In lesson 3, she buys and plants a garden. Gardening will build muscles because of the turning of the soil, making furrows, planting seeds, hoeing and watering.

To have this physical strength, women must keep their bodies in good physical condition—both inside and outside. To be active, they must have an abundance of vitality.

1. What is the definition of vitality? _____

_____

2. What is the definition of lethargy? _____

_____

Vitality catches the eye, lethargy repels the eye. To be attractive, a woman must look alive, feel alive and act alive—for life attracts life.

The devil would love to see a woman mistreat her body. He does not want her to have vitality that is pleasing to God and others. He would rather have her functioning on half the energy that could be hers if she would discipline herself to exercise and eat right. He would rather have her mind be sluggish and keep her from being mentally and spiritually alert. However, this is not what the Lord desires. He wants a woman to be alert and healthy so she can serve Him to her fullest capacity. There are some He chooses to suffer illness, but to most women the Lord has given a productive life. Do not disappoint Him by neglecting to take care of the body in which He dwells and through which He works.

To keep physically fit will take discipline—the training that develops self-control. Keeping physically fit isn't so difficult if you know what to do and how to do it.

3. Before discussing some daily exercises, answer the following questions regarding physical fitness:

In a standing position, can you long jump a distance equal to your body height? _____

Can you walk a mile in 15 minutes? _____

In a standing position, can you touch your toes with your fingertips, without bending your knees? _____

Can you do 20 sit-ups in a minute? _____

Are you ready to try out for the Olympics? If not, the following is one exercise method you may want to try:

Stretch—tiptoe around the room, reaching for the ceiling.
Bend—keep knees straight; touch your toes ten times.
Kick—holding on to a table, kick each leg back and forth.
Twist—stretch out arms; twist and bend to touch opposite toes.
Rock—sit with feet crossed, hands on knees, then rock on hips.
Bicycle—lie on floor, lift legs into the air, and with your hips
        propped with your hands, bicycle.

Another reason for exercise is to take away or add to those parts of the figure which are not properly proportioned. Exercising tears down cells, so if the cells are in the wrong place, tearing them down is good. Regular exercise can keep the cells torn down and discourage new layers. If you wish to add to a certain portion of the body, exercise vigorously for that area, then wait for a day or two before exercising again to allow cells to rebuild in that area. When trying to take off extra inches, regular, daily exercise must be maintained. Missing days in between will actually add cells to those areas.

4. Are you properly proportioned? Measure yourself and make notes beside each of the following areas. Indicate how much you want to add or subtract to your figure according to statistics from *Pattern for Living.*[1]

How do you measure up? Addition or subtraction of inches:

Your waist should be 10 inches less than your bust _____

Your hips should equal your bust _____

Your thighs should be 6 inches less than your waist _____

Your calves should be 6 inches less than your thighs _____

Your ankles should be 4 inches less than your calves _____

Another suggestion for exercise is to take up a sport on a regular basis to keep physically fit while adding or subtracting inches. Jogging for an hour can burn off 900 calories. Playing tennis for an hour takes care of 420 calories.

Exercise that stirs the blood and flexes the muscle tissue will leave its mark in a firm physique and also in a good mental attitude.

A balanced diet is very important to inward and outward beauty. Eat a variety of foods—green and yellow vegetables, meats, some carbohydrates, bread and cereals, fruit and milk products—every day. Remember, everything that goes inside shows on the outside—and not necessarily in weight only. Wholesome, nourishing food full of vitamins, minerals and proteins is necessary to produce clear skin, sparkling eyes, shining hair and gleaming teeth.

There are four basic food groups to use when planning menus for the family:

Meats—fish, chicken, beef, nuts, eggs and other protein foods.
Fruits and fruit juices, green and yellow vegetables.
Milk and milk products—cheese, butter, cottage cheese, etc.
Breads and cereals (preferably whole grain and not highly processed).

Some foods have no nutritional value except to add grease and carbohydrates to the diet. Unfortunately, in this category are potato chips, some Mexican foods, imitation and highly processed foods and soft drinks.

Also in caring for the body, preventative medicine is a must for every woman. Yearly physicals with breast examinations and pap tests should be scheduled.

What about appearance? How important is the physical appearance, or is it important at all?

The Christian women who are really being used of God are lovely ladies inwardly and outwardly. The subject of outward beauty has been misunderstood in Christian circles far too often. The Bible speaks often against pride and vanity regarding one's appearance, and as a result, many have concluded that outward beauty is undesirable. **The key to real beauty is a balance between the inward and the outward.** The ladies who are lovely inwardly should be lovely on the outside, too. First Samuel 16:7 says, "The Lord seeth not as man seeth; for man looketh on the outward appearance, but the Lord looketh on the heart."

It is true that God sees the inner beauty, inner motives, inner thoughts and dreams; but man has nowhere else to look but on the outward appearance.

When a man sees a woman, he looks first at her physical qualifications. It is a built-in, natural trait for him. He will look at her face and her figure (not necessarily in that order). If a woman possesses the virtuous inner qualities that come from God, man will see the shining reflection of God in her. It takes both the outward and inward qualities to complete a woman's picture. If she is warm, giving, alert, loving, fun to be with and has femininity that is uncommonly beautiful, plus being spiritual, there is nothing a man can say but "What a woman!"

The Biblical heroines are good examples of outward appearance pleasing to mankind and inward beauty pleasing to God. Sarah is recognized for her faith in Hebrews 11, yet she was so beautiful that Abraham worried about losing her to one of the kings. Rachel was always favored above Leah as Jacob's wife because of her physical beauty. Esther was so lovely that she was chosen from hundreds of women to be the queen.

Charm and beauty are demonstrated by not getting too wrapped up in the outward appearance, yet not ignoring it either. It is making the best of the original "equipment" that God designed and created. Obviously basic physical features cannot be changed. Attractiveness does not depend solely upon that with which one is born. A woman should not moan and groan because her complexion, hair and figure are not like her friend's. She can use her wits and will to improve her own figure, hair and complexion. Just for fun, spend an afternoon at the beauty shop and get a new hairdo. Also ask the beautician about what makeup is best for the skin.

5. Because people do look on the outward appearance, what are some steps to take toward outward beauty? (Suggestions from Joyce Landorf).

Clean Skin (Ruth 3:3a):
Bathe or shower daily; shave legs and underarms; apply deodorant. Applying your favorite perfume after bathing when pores are open keeps the fragrance lasting longer. Use cold or warm creams or lotions to get your face clean. Some beauty experts feel soap dries the natural oils and accelerates the aging process, so go easy on soap. Find the one that works for you and use it. After a good face cleaning, you might want to finish off with an astringent because it closes the pores.

Sensible Makeup:
Few of us have peaches-and-cream complexions—mostly we have red blotches, lines and circles under our eyes. Whether we use liquid, cream, tub, jar, stick or cake makeup, the point is to cover the blemishes without being too garish.

Eyes:
Our eyes are the "windows of our souls"; therefore, we should give them attention. Start at the top and work down.

1. Pluck out stray hairs from your eyebrows. You may need an eyebrow pencil or brush to fill in the sparse spots.
2. Eye shadow will add a soft, glowing sparkle to your eyes, but use it sparingly because you are not dressing for a circus.
3. If you do not have long curly eyelashes, you may want to invest in an eyelash curler and use mascara to thicken and darken your eyelashes.

Lips:
Find a shade of lipstick that softens or flatters your face and use it in good taste. The same goes for coloring your cheeks with blush; softness is the rule. Remember never to apply your makeup in public. Mend your face in the ladies' room.

Hair (Matthew 10:30):
Because the hairs of our heads are numbered, our hair must

be important to the Lord. Therefore, we must care for and maintain our hair. Keeping it clean with a quality shampoo and a conditioning rinse are basics. Find a hairdresser you feel is competent and get a good trim or have your hair styled as often as needed or as you can afford it.

Hands:

You may be able to keep some secrets up your sleeve, but not tell-tale hands. They stand out for all the world to see. Your hands should be soft and clean; fingernails should be smooth and shapely. The cuticles should be pushed back and hangnails removed; polish applied if desired.

Mouth:

"Bad breath is better than no breath" to you, but to the person with whom you are conversing, that may not be true. Brush your teeth after every meal and use a good mouthwash to help keep your breath sweet.

Clothing:

You should dress so that you are up-to-date, but not outlandish. Choose basic styles, learn to sew and avoid extremes. Dress with simplicity; become color-wise; mix and match with care; become a smart shopper by learning to recognize a bargain; read the labels regarding washing instructions; check the fit of a garment as well as the tailoring. Dress appropriately—the right clothes for the right occasion.[2]

There is a saying that clothes make the man—they also make the woman. Clothes indicate so much about a woman: her age, maturity, income, taste, background and job. This matter of how women dress is really an important issue and not to be taken lightly.

6. What does Jesus warn in Matthew 5:28? _____

_____

A woman should not dress in such a way as to cause a man to lust after her. If she does dress in this fashion, she is partly to blame for his thoughts and actions. A survey by Hollywood Social Studies was published with the following statistics: 90% believed girls wearing miniskirts risk increased danger of rape attack; 94% thought statistics showing increasing molestation of young girls might be caused by short dresses; 98% said provocative clothing might encourage men to sex crimes. Though statistics on forcible rape declined in the five-year period ending in 1963, they suddenly shot up in 1964; up 68% in the United States and 90% in England. The report said one factor could have been Mary Quant's introduction of the miniskirt. (Many will recall she designed it to announce that she was ready to go to bed with a man anytime, night or day.) The Hollywood Social Studies report concluded, "No other adequate cause for this strange reversal has been found."[3]

Recently, the style for the skirt length has gone below the knee, but it is not just a matter of a skirt length; often a neckline is too plunging, a blouse unbuttoned too low, a sweater too tight, a fabric too clinging.

Why are Christian women often careless in their dress? Maybe it is because they just do not think like men. God simply did not make their emotional responses like those of men. Women do not respond to the same kinds of stimuli a man does; therefore, it is often impossible for women to believe that what they wear could be that provocative or suggestive.

A woman is not ordinarily excited by sight. Normally, the sight of a nude male would not move her to passion. A woman responds to touch. A man's gentle hands would do more to give his wife a sense of total protection and arouse a responding love than any picture could do.

7. How can clothing betray one's spiritual condition (Prov. 23:7a)? _____

_____

_____

It is also true that the clothing a woman wears can affect how she feels. Little girls like to "dress up" in Mommy's dresses because the pretty clothes make them feel pretty.

This is one reason the Lord took so much time in the Bible to describe how brides adorn themselves for their husbands. Except for salvation, no other experience of life is as lasting and far-reaching in consequence as marriage. It is right for a bride to spend time and thought in getting her bridal clothes ready. They add to the sense of the importance of the event.

How a woman dresses and conducts herself will also determine the character of her performance. She acts differently in a dress than she does in slacks. In a dress a woman is more ladylike, but in slacks she is apt to be more relaxed; therefore, she needs to be careful how she sits and walks. Not only clothing gives a message to a man but also the way a woman walks, moves her body, her hands and feet. A man may expect a woman to sell what she advertises. If she does not want to be propositioned, then she should not advertise.

Review the verses in lesson 1 that deal with the evil woman. The harlot's attire is described in some of those verses. Her clothing is anything that accents the physical features, the secret parts of the body. A virtuous woman does not wear such clothing—her clothes show her modest character.

Recently in an office, a repair person (female) was working on a Xerox machine. She was wearing a jumpsuit. With all the bending and stooping she was doing, she probably thought a jumpsuit was proper attire. However, because of the form fit of the suit, it was obvious to all who saw her that, under her outfit, she was wearing bikini panties.

Another incident occurred when several couples were enjoying homemade ice cream one summer evening. The hostess was attired in white shorts with a blouse tied in a knot at the waist. Again, it was obvious she was wearing bikini panties—blue ones! It was embarrassing to the other women guests. Ladies, if wearing slacks, be careful how tightly they fit, what is worn underneath them and the occasion for which they are worn.

8. Ask your husband (father, if you are single) if there are some clothes he would rather you did not wear to church, to the office or to go shopping. He knows how other men think and how they will react to your wardrobe. Now check your wardrobe to see if any of your dresses, blouses, sweaters or slacks are:

____ too tight	____ too suggestive
____ too short	____ not your color
____ too revealing	____ not your style

9. Write out the Scripture verse that goes with the following guidelines for good grooming for Christian women.

Strive to please God in everything—including actions and dress (1 Cor. 10:31). _____

_____

Dress with style and taste so your appearance will bring honor to the One you represent (2 Cor. 5:20). _____

_____

Avoid gaudy clothing and makeup, realizing that this will focus too much attention on the outer appearance and dim the beauty of Christ within (Gal. 2:20). _____

_____

Use moderation in fashion—neither "old-fashioned" nor "first in fashion" (Phil. 4:5). _____

_____

Be stylish when possible, but refuse to lower standards just to conform to the crowd (Rom. 12:2). _____

_____

(1 Thess. 5:21) _____

_____

Clothing should not be for vainglory and show (Phil. 2:3).

_____

Standing before a mirror, ask yourself, "Would I want to meet Jesus looking like this?" (1 Thess. 2:4). _____

_____

Strive to look feminine— be proud God made you a woman (Deut. 22:5). _____

Do not "play up your sex" lest you be labeled cheap or common (1 Cor. 6:20). _____

_____

Modesty in appearance brings God's approval as well as man's (Prov. 31:10, 11). _____

10. What is taught in 1 Timothy 2:9, 10? _____

11. What is Peter's admonition in 1 Peter 3:3, 4? _____

It is necessary to understand that a Hebrew idiom has been used in the two previous verses (1 Pet. 3:3, 4). According to Ralph Woodrow in his book, *Women's Adornment,* "An idiom is a manner of speaking distinctively of a certain people or language. In this case, the idiom was a manner of speaking which would emphasize a second clause. Today in order to express the thought contained in this type of idiom, we would place the word 'only' in the first clause, and 'also' (or perhaps 'rather') in the second clause as follows: 'Let not a woman's adornment be [only] that of outward things—such as fixing her hair, wearing gold, or pearls, or apparel—but [also/rather] let it be the inward adorning of a meek and quiet spirit' (1 Peter 3:3). With this idiom, the emphasis is on the second clause, but it does not do away with the first clause, it is in addition to it."[4]

The word "sobriety" in 1 Timothy 2:9 means "prudence" or "moderation." Women are to clothe themselves in modest apparel in moderation.

No amount of makeup or mascara, a fancy hairdo or expensive clothes can cover the fact that a woman is not getting enough rest or proper foods. Some ladies can get by with six hours of sleep, while others require seven or eight hours. Continual lack of sleep robs ladies of their beauty and radiance.

12. List improvements you would like to make in your appearance:

_____

_____

In Proverbs 31:23, the way a married woman looks, dresses and acts can affect how other people feel about her husband: *"Her husband is known in the gates, when he sitteth among the elders of the land."*

This may sound like her husband goes out after dinner, sits with the other men on the benches along Main Street and "shoots the breeze" while his wife is slaving away at the dinner dishes. However, this is not so. In Bible times, the gate of the city was a place of much activity. This Proverbs man has a well-known, reputable name, for he sits with the elders of the land who are chosen into the council of the city as the chief place of the land, and he has a great deal of influence in his position. The elders meet and discuss the law and politics (Ruth 4:1). The Proverbs lady has a husband who is involved in these procedures and has even gained a good reputation for himself. The idea is that because of his wife, the husband has risen to a place of prominence in the city (Prov. 12:4).

A husband who has a wife who lives a chaste life, and who sends him off to work neat and clean and with a happy heart, will show results in his work. This is the kind of wife every Christian woman should strive to be. Because she is a good homemaker, her husband is able to fulfill his obligations. Behind every successful man is a diligent woman. Even more important than civic and social obligations to a man are his obligations to the Lord. In some areas of Christian service, it is impossible for a man to function as he should without a spiritually-minded wife who is able and willing to work with him (Titus 2:4, 5).

After looking at several aspects of a woman's outward beauty, now consider her inner beauty. Proverbs 31:10 says the godly woman is virtuous—meaning she exhibits many beneficial qualities which include modesty, decency and trustworthiness. The 25 th verse tells how others see her: *"Strength and honor are her clothing; and she shall rejoice in time to come."* The Hebrew word for strength, *owz,* used in verse 17 as well as 25 means strength in various applications—force, majesty, praise and security.

In this 25th verse, all the facade is stripped away and the virtuous woman is shown for what she really is. Others see in her that inner strength, the strength that is of the mind—the power over the changes of temporal circumstances which easily shatter and bring ruin to a household laid on less solid foundations. Not only does this woman have a good self-image, but she is consistent in her thoughts and actions. She has a proper mental attitude in trials and in disappointments. This strength comes from inside. She has stored up the wonderful promises of God and rests in faith on those promises. As a result, she wears as her clothing, honor. This raiment represents true pride and true dignity with which she can look confidently into the future, armed against sorrow and care. She is dressed with splendor, majesty and glory.

The strength of this outfit was designed in Heaven, not in Paris or Hollywood. The poor can enjoy clothing made of these eternal fabrics—strength and honor—the same as the rich. Regardless of a woman's income or circumstances, she can learn to dress herself in this strength and honor if her heart is actively tuned toward God. This strength is the inner steel that gives a woman character, regardless of her physical condition. It is the resiliency that allows her to cope with her ever-changing circumstances. It is the determination that shapes her life and the lives of those around her.

Character in no way attacks femininity—it enhances it. Strength of character comes from waiting on the Lord through daily communication with Him (Isa. 40:28-31). Femininity is a woman's crowning glory in her attitude of honor, self-control, virtue, chastity, purity, a clean heart, sweetness, a gentle and quiet spirit and modesty.

In 1 Timothy 4:8 we are told bodily exercise is profitable, but spiritual exercise is more important.

13. What do the following verses indicate regarding the necessity of a daily "spiritual beauty treatment"?

Appetite for God's Word (1 Pet. 2:2). _____

_____

Feeding on God's Word (Matt. 4:4). _____

_____

Storing God's Word (Ps. 119:11). _____

_____

14. God's Word will provide the necessary ingredients for a healthy spiritual body. What are these food items?

Deuteronomy 8:3 _____

Psalm 119:103 _____

Ephesians 5:26 _____

1 Peter 2:2 _____

Hebrews 5:12-14 _____

The following chart by Dr. Elmer W. Palmer compares the physical life with the spiritual life of a Christian.[5]

PHYSICAL	SPIRITUAL

1. Breathe
   Normal
   Not difficult
	1. Pray
	   Always (Luke 18:1)
	   Unhindered by sin
	   (1 Peter 3:7)

2. Eat · daily	2. Read the Bible daily (Acts 17:11)

3. Exercise
   Use arms and legs or
   they become useless
	3. Live for Jesus
	   At home, school, work,
	   play—everywhere

The physical life for everyone demands three things: to breathe, to eat, to exercise. These three things are also necessary for the spiritual life. If there has been no prayer to God for salvation, there is no spiritual life. To have spiritual strength, a Christian must read the Bible daily. There are many Christians who are defeated and live weak lives because they do not feed on the Word of God. It is necessary that the Bible be read every day just as it is necessary to eat every day. A good motto is, "No Bible, no breakfast."

Exercise is a must to keep physically strong. If one does not use the arm and leg muscles, these muscles will soon atrophy. All the body needs to be exercised in some way every day.

The same is true with the Christian. What exercise is to the body, living for Jesus is to the spiritual life. Others should see by a woman's actions Christ living in her. Remember the words of James Rowe:

Earthly pleasures vainly call me, I would be like Jesus,
Nothing worldly shall enthrall me, I would be like Jesus.
Be like Jesus, this my song, In the home and in the throng;
Be like Jesus, all day long! I would be like Jesus.

In the natural, physical life, it is common sense to breathe,
eat and exercise. In the spiritual life it is common sense to pray,
read the Bible daily and live for Jesus.

If a man does not exercise his arm, he develops no biceps muscle, and if a man does not exercise his soul, he acquires no muscle
in his soul, no strength of character, no vigor of moral fiber, nor
beauty of spiritual growth.

Henry Drummond

Along with this strength of character goes dignity. Dignity is
honor, worthiness, calm self-respect. Mistakes are made and
dignity helps a person get through the embarrassment of the
mistakes. Dignity helps a woman stand tall when she would really
rather run and hide. As a Christian woman, this sense of dignity
is based on her relationship to Jesus Christ. She is clothed in His
righteousness as well as with the armor of His protection. Because
of His presence in her life, she can stand straight and tall.

"She shall rejoice in time to come" refers to the future. The
Proverbs lady rejoices or smiles at the future. Why? Because she
and her family are prepared for the future, no matter what happens. She does not go around biting her fingernails because she
knows her family's spiritual destiny, and she knows the Lord is
going to provide for them in the material sense. Having lived in
the fear of God and honored God with the fruits of righteousness,
there is sunshine in her hour of trial, "in the valley of the shadow
of death," in the unclouded day of eternity when she shall be
welcomed "into the joy of the Lord." Therefore, she has a proper
mental attitude toward the future and has no fear.

Thoughts of fear about the future may cause women to have
uncertainties—unemployment, crime, famine, wars, ERA, rights
for homosexuals, etc.

15. Joyce Landorf has some tips to help women cope with fear. The first step is to make a list of the things that cause fear. ____

Jesus said people would never be free from problems and fear, but He has promised to help overcome these (John 16:33). Psychologists and doctors agree that until a person finds out what ails him, he cannot be cured. Mental health begins by admitting and then accepting all the facts of one's life.

The second step in coping with fear is to find out where the fear originates and stop the source.

16. What do the following verses tell us?

2 Timothy 1:7 _____

1 John 4:8, 18 _____

When a woman has that first thought of fear, she should remember it is not from God. Satan gets the credit for inventing the power of suggestion, and he uses it cleverly to attack Christians. He knows the name of every born-again Christian. He also knows he cannot take Christ away from a Christian or steal a Christian's salvation, but he does his best to defeat and discourage Christians. Satan finds a woman's particular panic button and presses as hard as he can. He may use the fear of breast cancer or the fear of being an "old maid" or even of becoming a widow. When he finds that fear, he will make it his biggest weapon for damaging mental health, confident outward composure, and victorious Christian living.

When Satan plants this fear in a woman, he then sits back and watches her fight it. He gets her to spend her waking hours and most of her sleeping hours troubled over the fear. He delights in robbing her of one of her most priceless possessions—time.

Satan used Scripture when he tempted Jesus, so Christians today are no exceptions to this rule. Satan twisted God's words to Eve in the Garden of Eden, and she fell for it.

Here is a basic rule of thumb in determining the difference between God's suggestions and Satan's (Phil. 4:8; James 3:17).

If the thought is from the Lord it always will be
Honest—not scrambled in any way

Pure—no ulterior motives
Kind and good—not destructive
   If the thought is from Satan it is probably
A lie—even a little white one (they turn into big black ones)
A deception—the truth twisted very cleverly
A destructive suggestion that will hurt

    A third step in coping with fear is to determine who controls a woman's life. It is a matter of choice and she must decide. Paul talks of people who are still under the control of their old sinful natures in the flesh (before they became Christians) and that they can never please God.

    17. What does Paul tell the new Christians in Romans 8:9?

_____

    The answer to living with fear is found in the woman's soul. The secret of victory is not found in her struggling alone with that fear but willingly letting Christ take that fear and leaving it with Him. This way she decides who controls her life—Christ, not Satan.

    18. What is Peter's warning in 1 Peter 5:8? _____

_____

    Taking these three steps regarding fear will help a woman to have that inner peace and be the beautiful, glowing woman God would have her to be.
Bring your fears honestly before the Lord by writing them on a sheet of paper, and leave the list with Him.

Know your enemy is Satan. He is the author of all fearful thoughts.

Decide exactly *who* will control the body, soul and mind. [6]

    19. What encouragement is stated in 1 John 4:4? _____

_____

    For women, getting older is probably one of their biggest fears; but if God is able to guide at 18, 25 and 32, He can do the same at 45, 60 and 80. With Jesus Christ in a woman's life, every year should become "Sweeter as the Years go By." At any given time she is the age God purposed her to be, according to His pattern. Dale Evans Rogers says, "Age is a matter of an attitude of mind and heart." The Proverbs lady looks forward to the future with happy anticipation—it is part of her "positive thinking." It actually makes her prettier because it puts the lines on her face in the right places. By accepting the wrinkles, corns, backaches, gray hairs and bifocals as God's gradual refining for Heaven, women will be able to gracefully walk along with strength and honor as God planned.

20. What special tasks does the Lord have for older people?

Psalm 78:3-7 _____

Joel 1:2, 3 _____

1 Timothy 5:9, 10 _____

Titus 2:1-5 _____

21. Women need God's strength and power for inner beauty.

What does Psalm 90:17 say? _____

_____

22. Where does the strength for inner beauty come from (Phil. 4:13)? _____

23. What other qualities for inner beauty can women claim?

Psalm 94:19 _____

Psalm 46:1, 2 _____

John 14:27 _____

John 16:33 _____

NO GOD—NO PEACE.   KNOW GOD—KNOW PEACE.

The crooked teeth, the acne-scarred complexion or the swollen arthritic hands do not really matter. To be truly beautiful, look into the face of the Lord Jesus, then reflect His love and compassion to a world that is dying.

> Let the beauty of Jesus be seen in me.
> All His wonderful passion and purity;
> O Thou Spirit divine,
> All my nature refine,
> Till the beauty of Jesus is seen in me.

Albert Orsborn

PERSONAL APPLICATION

Now that you have a pattern for inward and outward beauty, you should be able to take this quiz by answering true or false.

1. I have taken a shower or bath today. _____

2. My hairdo looks nice right now. _____

3. My nails are manicured. _____

4. My makeup looks natural and has a touch of color. _____

5. My wardrobe includes only things that look good on me and fit me properly. _____

6. Nothing in my wardrobe is immodest in any way. _____

7. The jewelry I am wearing complements and accents my outfit. _____

8. I exercise at least five minutes daily. _____

9. (If married) My husband is able to perform "in the gates" because I am fulfilling my role (Titus 2:4, 5). _____

10. I have a daily "spiritual beauty treatment." _____
(One way to begin a daily devotional time is to secure a copy of *Our Daily Bread* from Radio Bible Class, Grand Rapids, Michigan.)

11. I take my fears to the Lord and leave them with Him. ____

12. I will memorize Philippians 4:13. _____

NOTES

1. Joy Erdman, *Pattern for Living* (Crown Point, IN: Christian Womanhood, 1977), 60.

2. Joyce Landorf, *Fragrance of Beauty* (Wheaton, IL: Victor Books, 1973), 44-46.

3. Elizabeth Rice Handford, *Your Clothes Say It For You* (Murfreesboro, TN: Sword of the Lord Publishers, 1976), 72, 73.

4. Ralph Woodrow, *Women's Adornment* (Riverside, CA: 1976), 20, 21.

5. Elmer W. Palmer, *So A Child May Understand* (Eaton, CO: First Baptist Church, 1966), 17-19.

6. Landorf, 30-34.

Lesson 5

PATTERN FOR STEWARDSHIP

She perceiveth that her merchandise is good: her candle goeth not out by night (Proverbs 31:18).

THE HEBREW WORD *taam,* for "perceiveth," means to taste. Today a woman would say to discern or realize. She tests her cooking by tasting a bit of what she is preparing.

This Proverbs lady periodically takes the time to test her gain from her work and is careful to consider that her motivation is right, that she does her work all for the glory and honor of God and not out of selfishness. Her merchandise is profit or gain from her work. She passes the test for her gain is good; she knows gratification because she sees her business ventures bring her gain. A quote from the Keil and Delitsch Commentary is: "She comes to find (taste) how profitable her industry is by experience resulting from the sale of its product: the corn, the grapes, and the wine are found to be good, and thus her gain is better. This spurs on her active industry to redoubled effort and at times, when she is not fully occupied by oversight of her fields and vineyards, she has another employment over which her light goes not out till far in the night."[1]

She runs her business on a balanced budget—an accomplishment that is reached by few governments! She gets good things, in fact, the best, because she knows the value of money and how to spend it. However, she would rather do without some things than to burden her family with difficult installments and get them into debt.

One would think this woman is a magician because she has learned to make old things look new again. It is not surprising to know that she can prepare a lovely meal from leftovers. The word "waste" is not in her vocabulary (waste not—want not). Benjamin Franklin said, "A penny saved is a penny earned," and this statement is a thrifty reality in the home of God's ideal woman.

Today's Christian woman should be watchful in her work and see that she performs her duties as unto the Lord and that she is not wasteful with the material possessions the Lord has given her. How a woman perceives her merchandise is demonstrated in the way she acts as a steward of what God has given her. The definition of a steward according to the dictionary is "a person put in charge of the affairs of a large household or estate, whose duties include supervision and management; one who acts as an administrator for others." A steward is one who owns nothing but is responsible for everything entrusted to his care. As children of God, Christians are His agents and part of their calling lies in the management of His property.

Christian stewards must realize that they live, and move, and have their being in Jesus Christ. They are not their own because they are bought with the price of His blood shed on the cross for their sins. The whole of the Christian's life—personality, time, talent, influence, material substance, everything—must be dedicated to Christ. He is also the Pattern for Christians to follow for perfect stewardship.

1. What does Romans 14:12 tell us? _____

_____

2. List the acts of Christ in His stewardship that demonstrate His perfection (Phil. 2:5-9). _____

_____

3. What was Christ's supreme purpose in life (John 6:38)?

_____

Stewardship of a Woman's Body

4. For Whom are we a steward (1 Cor. 6:19, 20)? _____

_____

5. We are a steward of our _____ (James 3:2-5). Why is it such an important member of our body (James 3:6)?

_____

What should we know concerning its use (Matt. 12:36)? _____

_____

6. We are also a steward of our _____ (Prov. 4:23).
What should we know about it (Jer. 17:9)? _____

_____

What should a steward of God continually pray (Ps. 139:23, 24)? _____

_____

What condition of heart does God require (Ps. 51:17)? _____

_____

7. We are a steward of our _____ (1 Pet. 1:13).
Whose mind should we have as a faithful steward of God's grace (Phil. 2:5-8)? _____

What is the result of keeping our minds stayed on God (Isa. 26:3)? _____

_____

How do we keep our minds on Him (Phil. 4:6, 7)? _____

_____

Stewardship of a Woman's Time

Since God is the Lord of a Christian's life, He is also the Lord of hours and days. Each one is precious, for it can only be lived once. The hours may be lived victoriously, fellowshipping with God, or the time may be squandered. Each lady alone is the steward of her time. Paul said, "Whatsoever ye do, do all to the glory of God" (1 Cor. 10:31). David, in Psalm 31:15, stated, "My times are in thy hand."

Perhaps one of the hardest things to define is time. One reason may be that there is no time with God and there will be no time in eternity. A well-known preacher made this comment about time: "The older I get the more I realize that perhaps the greatest gift I could give you is my time. Actually, the only gift that I can give you is my time. If I give you money, I give you the time it took me to earn that money. If I give you a gift, I give you the time it took me to earn the money with which I bought the gift. Perhaps, then, it is true that time is the only thing that I can really give to you."

8. Explain Colossians 4:5. _____

_____

9. What should be our prayer concerning the use of the time that God gives us (Ps. 90:12)? _____

_____

10. As good stewards, what will we do (Eph. 5:15, 16)? _____

_____

How certain is this time and why (James 4:14)? _____

_____

What does God demand of women as stewards of their time (Ps. 62:8)? _____

11. As wise stewards concerned about the use of our time, we want to understand:
The Holy Spirit will enable the faithful steward to perform the duties of stewardship by giving _____ (Acts 1:8).
What our attitude will be as we utilize the time of which God has made us to be stewards (Eph. 5:19, 20). _____

_____

_____

Stewardship of a Woman's Talents and Gifts

The Bible refers to the Church as the Body of Christ. Christ is the Head (1 Cor. 12:27; Eph. 5:23). Just as the body has many specialized parts, each having its own function, so the Church is composed of many individuals, each with his or her own special function and contribution to the rest of the Body.

Every Christian possesses both natural and spiritual gifts. All people have natural gifts (abilities and talents) that they are born with. Some ladies enjoy creating lovely flower arrangements, while others design dresses, raise vegetables, entertain, write humorous notes or use their musical abilities. Almost every woman has a hobby or something she enjoys and does well.

12. What talents and natural abilities do you have? _____

_____

13. How would you apply Colossians 3:17 to the stewardship of your natural gifts? _____

Every Christian has at least one spiritual gift that is imparted to him by the Holy Spirit at the Christian's spiritual birth. These gifts enable Christians to minister to others in behalf of Christ.

14. What instruction is given in 1 Peter 4:10? _____

_____

15. Make a list of the spiritual gifts in Romans 12:3-8, 1 Corinthians 12:1-31, Ephesians 4:11, 12 and 1 Peter 4:10, 11.

_____

_____

_____

_____

16. List the principles concerning your attitude and responsibility toward your gift (Rom. 12:3-8). _____

_____

17. What is your spiritual gift(s)? _____
18. How can you minister to others with your spiritual gift?

_____

_____

Stewardship of a Woman's Possessions

19. What did God command those under the law of Moses to do in Malachi 3:8-10? _____

20. According to Hebrews 7:2, how much is a tithe? _____

Believers in Christ are not under the Law, they are under

grace. The Law in itself did not provide eternal life for those who attempted to keep it (Gal. 2:16; 3:21, 22). Christians have received life by the grace of God, though they do not deserve it and could not possibly earn it. Therefore, Christians have a higher motivation and standard for stewardship of their possessions than those who were under the Law.

21. The following verses provide two examples of giving:

2 Corinthians 8:9 _____

2 Corinthians 9:15 _____

22. What kind of giver does God love (2 Cor. 9:7)? _____

After reading all the Scripture verses for today's lesson, a woman can see that God really cares about her as an individual. He is concerned about how she uses her tongue, her heart-condition, her mind, body, gifts and possessions. He has given her all these things. It saddens God's heart when she belittles herself complaining that she has no talent, that she is not creative or intelligent or pretty. God made each woman the way she is and when she puts herself down, she is insulting God. She needs to accept her abilities and limitations as God's design for her while at the same time remembering God loves her because she is created in His image.

How does the subject of stewardship fit into a woman's daily life? It is often said, "There just aren't enough hours in the day." This seems to be true for women in these helter-skelter days. To be a good steward of her life, a woman needs to first establish a daily schedule by establishing priorities, recording her plan of action and then sticking to the plan.

23. What are some possible steps to take in planning a daily schedule?

In a small notebook that will fit into your purse, write down the things you have to do today: Getting the family off to work or school, making beds, running errands, preparing meals, cleaning up afterwards and making time for yourself with the Lord or relaxing. Keep a calendar close at hand to record meetings and appointments. These are routine but necessary for daily living.

Assign a priority to every item on your list. Tackle hard jobs early in the day when you are fresh and alert.

What you do not get done today, put on your list for tomorrow.

Do not worry if you cannot complete everything on your list in one day. Look at all the things you did complete!

One secret of being a good steward of time is knowing what has to be done and how to do it; another secret is getting at the job and doing it (Prov. 16:3). Attitude is half the work. This calls for sorting priorities and putting first things first.

Writing out a time schedule in the notebook may be helpful. Indicate what needs to be done in a certain time block, including appointments and meetings. Every woman needs to plan her schedule to suit herself and the family needs. Sticking to a schedule requires effort, self-discipline and a "want to" attitude.

The home is the most important social unit in society. As goes the home, so goes the community, the church and the nation. Homemakers need to learn to do everything (dishes, ironing, diapers, mopping, cleaning the toilet bowl, cooking, helping husband and children) "as unto Him." Whatever is done, whether it is eating, drinking, working or playing, it should be to the honor and glory of God.

In Proverbs 31:18, the pattern lady is very economical in her stewardship of finances because her merchandise brings her gain. Someone has said, "Money is a universal passport to everywhere, except to Heaven, and is the provider of everything but happiness."

Money Will Buy . . .

A bed but not sleep.
Books but not brains.
Food but not appetite.
Finery but not beauty.
A house but not a home.
Medicine but not health.
Luxuries but not culture.
Amusement but not happiness.
Religion but not salvation.[2]

Money can be a medium of exchange for the necessities of life, or it can be one's master, controlling the life. Money is often a major cause in quarrels between couples. It is also a chief cause of divorce. Why is this a real problem in today's homes?

Lack of training in how to spend money by shopping wisely may be one reason. "Easy credit" is a major cause of driving families to financial failure. Excessive spending for bigger and better cars, expensive restaurants and expensive gifts is another problem.

An authority on finances gives advice on how to get out of debt and stay out: "Work out a hardcore budget and stick to it." He says to stick to the basic needs—food, clothing, housing and medical care. By doing this, families and individuals will be amazed at the large amount of nonessential spending that has been done.

24. What are some ways women can economize as good stewards?

Know your product and its quality, and compare prices.

Buy during seasonal sales at reliable stores.

Secondhand furniture is a good investment for young couples. If a piece of furniture needs refinishing, this can be a fun family project and very rewarding.

Do without some items for the time being.

Be creative by using your own skills: make curtains from towels or sheets; sew for your family (anything from slippers to ski jackets and sleeping bags can be sewn at home); do your own decorating—decoupage; dried flower arrangements in a bottle with a ribbon around it; get starter plants from friends.

"Brown bag" your lunch to the office instead of going out to eat.

Take advantage of free community services for education and recreation: concerts, parks, libraries, lectures, recreational centers, art exhibits.

Earn extra money without taking a job outside the home: bake wedding cakes, sew for others, babysit, type papers.

25. How can money be deceitful (1 Tim. 6:10)? _____

_____

Basic attitudes toward money and the things it can buy will determine how people live—within a budget based on income, or constantly in debt. Often, the amount of money people have is not the problem.

Another attitude to think about is wants versus needs. Television, newspapers and magazines want to convince people that what they do not have, they should buy. These ads may be especially geared toward women—perfume, clothes, furniture. Women need to ask God to help them sort wants from needs.

The attitude of making the most of what one has is essential. Ladies also need to learn to be content with what they have. Life does not consist only of possessions—it consists of relationships to God and others; feelings, emotions, goals, adventure, accomplishment, obedience to God and faithfulness to Him and to each other.

An appreciative wife is an encouragement to her husband when she is a good steward of the home and finances. She lets him know his efforts to provide for the family are truly appreciated and that his long hours and routine work are not in vain. A husband is more apt to enjoy his job and to work all the harder when he knows his wife thinks he is the greatest. This attitude helps to bring him straight home after work.

The husband should have the final decision in how the money is to be spent. His wife may be the better financier of the two; however, if she is to manage the budget, it should be his decision for her to do it.

Make money a servant, not a master. To do this, goals and priorities must be defined in establishing proper attitudes toward money and the things money can buy.

Using money as a blessing to others and to God brings contentment and happiness to you.

26. What is God's promise in Philippians 4:19? _____

_____

27. What is God's promise in Matthew 6:33? _____

_____

The last part of verse 18 states that *" her candle goeth not out by night."* Many women groan when they read this because it appears that a good wife will get up early and stay up half the night. Many do this, but it is not taught as the ideal here. The type of lamp used in those days required a constant supply of oil so that it would not go out and become smokey and difficult to relight. A wise woman checked the oil supply in the lamps before she went to bed. She planned ahead.

When daylight is over, the Proverbs lady does not call it quits. She stretches out the day with the use of candlelight. She uses the time to get things done, or else spends the time with the family discussing the day's events, or perhaps studies the Bible to orient her mind and will to what God would have her do.

Sometimes women get so involved (or behind) in their work that they feel that they are burning the candle at both ends. Even in this, moderation and balance are the key so their light will not flicker and dim prematurely.

Remember the Sunday School song, "This little light of mine, I'm going to let it shine." This light is a testimony to the world. The light of a woman's life shines out to others as they see her, and the world can tell if she is being a good steward of her time and talents (Matt. 5:16).

PERSONAL APPLICATION

1. Make a list of your stewardship responsibilities. _____

_____

2. Purchase a "daily planner" and begin recording appointments and meetings, shopping, cleaning, etc.

3. A helpful book regarding family finances is *You Can Be Financially Free* by George Fooshee.

Use the following chart for stewardship of your time. Fill in the hours spent for sleeping, cooking, cleaning, studying, errands, employment, eating, Christian service, rest, recreation, etc. Place total hours per week in each activity at the bottom of the chart. By listing the totals you can then discover if you have achieved the balanced use of time as a good steward.

HOUR	MON	TUES	WED	THURS	FRI	SAT	SUN
6:00							
7:00							
8:00							
9:00							
10:00							
11:00							
12:00							
1:00							
2:00							
3:00							
4:00							
5:00							
6:00							
7:00							
8:00							
9:00							
10:00							
11:00							
12:00							

Stewardship of Time

Sleeping ____ *Cooking* ____ *Cleaning* ____ *Studying* ____

Eating ____ *Errands* ____ *Employment* ____ *Christian Service*

____ *Rest* ____ *Recreation* ____ *Miscellaneous* ____

NOTES

1. C. F. Keil and F. Delitzsch, *Commentary on the Old Testament* (Grand Rapids: Wm. Eerdmans Publishing Company, 1975), 331.

2. Ella May Miller, *The Joy of Housekeeping* (Old Tappan, NJ: Fleming H. Revell, 1975), 83.

Lesson 6

PATTERN FOR SERVING

She stretcheth out her hand to the poor; yea, she reacheth forth her hands to the needy (Proverbs 31:20).

Paras, the Hebrew word for *"stretcheth,"* means to disperse, scatter or spread. In this verse, the pattern lady is intent upon giving. She often serves the poor and she does it freely, cheerfully and very liberally with an outstretched hand. Notice she not only relieves her poor neighbors and those who are close at hand, but she reaches out to the needy who are at a distance, seeking opportunities to do good.

The neighbors cannot be blamed for loving her. The aged, sick and shut-ins find her to be their best friend. She is never too busy with her own affairs to go to the assistance of others. She seems to know when someone is in need and either takes or sends the necessities. Her words bring comfort, hope and cheer to many people along life's pathway.

Up until now this lady has seemed to be "Hyper Hazel," rising when it is still dark, burning the midnight oil and spinning yarn on the distaff. One of the reasons for all this is so she can spread her gain and works to the poor. Because she is not entirely wrapped up in her own world and her own family, she is not blind to what is going on around her.

Welfare programs and food stamps were not necessary in Bible times because people cared for and helped to meet the needs of each other. There were certain rules regarding the poor in the Old Testament so that the poor could take care of themselves to a certain degree. Leviticus 19:10 records, "And thou shalt not glean thy vineyard, neither shalt thou gather every grape of thy vineyard; thou shalt leave them for the poor and stranger: I am the Lord your God."

President Ronald Reagan said that "all government welfare programs could be eliminated if churches would care for an average of ten families." If churches who were financially able to carry out a program such as this would do so, perhaps more nonbelievers would respond to the gospel. They would see that God's love truly benefits others (John 3:16).

The Proverbs lady is ready to reach out her hands to the needy, whether in body, mind or spirit. Not only is she generous in giving food and clothing, but with her own hands she ministers to the less fortunate. She is like a merchant ship, going to far places to bring back goods. She will also go to far places to help those in need. Because of her diligence and economy through her stewardship, the family has plenty for its own needs and she is able to minister this loving care to the poor and needy.

The hands of the Christian woman of today should also help those who are poor and needy. This is one way she can serve Christ. The hands that give to the needy are beautiful hands.

There is a legend of three young women who disputed who had the most beautiful hands. Each one did what she could to make her hands beautiful. A careworn, aged woman came asking a gift and each young woman refused her. A fourth young woman who made no claim to beauty ministered to the woman's need. The aged woman then said that the most beautiful hands were those that gave to the poor, and as she spoke, her mask fell off, her wrinkles disappeared and she stood before them, an angel of God.

Because it is more blessed to give than to receive (Acts 20:35), look at the characteristics of giving from the Scripture.

1. What is the Biblical principle for giving in Proverbs 3:9, 10? _____

_____

2. Since we have received freely from God, what should we do (Matt. 10:8b)? _____

3. Name one test of whether or not the love of God dwells in a person (1 John 3:17). _____

4. Another vital principle is found in 2 Corinthians 9:6. ____

_____

5. What does the Lord promise in Luke 6:38? _____

_____

6. Hebrews 6:10 tells what God will never forget. _____

_____

7. What is one condition of having the full blessing of God upon our lives (Isa. 58:10, 11)? _____

8. What is one way of discovering real happiness (Prov. 14:21)? _____

_____

9. What is one doing when he has pity on the needy (Prov. 19:17)? _____

_____

10. Name one way of overcoming enemies (Prov. 25:21, 22).

_____

_____

11. In time of trouble, what does God promise to do for the one who considers the poor (Ps. 41:1)? _____

_____

12. What is one way to merit true honor before men (Ps. 112:9)? _____

_____

13. How is this Christian ministry recorded in Heaven (Matt. 25:40)? _____

_____

Review some of the Scriptures in last week's lesson on giving to the Lord (Mal. 3:8; Prov. 3:9; 2 Cor. 9:7).

David said in Psalm 40:8, "I delight to do thy will, O my God." As a woman grows in appreciation of what God has done in her life through Jesus Christ at Calvary, she will long to do His will and serve and please Him in every way she can.

What would it have been like to live when Jesus walked this earth? Mary and Martha enjoyed the opportunity of opening their home to Him. Mary anointed Jesus' feet with her perfume. Women are the only people mentioned in the Bible as giving anything to Jesus. After His death on the cross, Joseph of Arimathea came forward to offer his tomb, but nowhere else is it recorded that an individual man actually performed a personal service to the Lord.

Each Christian woman has a definite place in serving. Jesus is the Supreme Example of a perfect servant; He lived to serve the Father.

14. Mark 10:45 tells why Jesus came to earth. _____

_____

15. Describe the acceptable service in these verses:

Romans 1:9 _____

2 Timothy 1:3 _____

16. What kind of heart attitude does God desire we possess as we enter into service for Him?

Psalm 2:11 _____

Psalm 100:2 _____

Acts 20:19 _____

Colossians 3:23 _____

17. Why does God want us to have these attitudes (Col. 3:24)? _____

_____

18. According to Galatians 5:13, what are Christians to do?

_____

The more a woman yields her life to the Holy Spirit, the more love she will have for God; consequently, her capacity for love and service will grow. God is loving others through her; she is seeing others through His eyes. He is ministering to them, but He is using her yielded personality, will and body to do so.

19. What does Jesus say in John 12:26? _____

_____

Now the question arises, Where is Jesus when He says, "Where I am, there shall also my servant be"? Because He is omnipresent, He is everywhere. He is present when there is a need—a sick friend, a new Christian who needs counseling, unsaved loved ones, sorrow—the list is never ending. Jesus is still serving others today, but He has chosen to serve through Christians. Christian women can meet the needs of others as Jesus ministers through them.

20. What will the Father do as we minister to others according to John 12:26? _____

This is exciting! The Lord not only has given everything of Himself at Calvary (redemption, eternal life, the promises of His care, guidance and assistance), but now in John 12:26 He says the Father will honor His servant. What an opportunity to serve the gracious Lord. The short time on this earth is to be lived as a time of preparation for what the Lord has waiting in Heaven.

21. What else will we be doing as we continue on with the Lord Jesus Christ in eternity (Rev. 22:3)? _____

We cannot be prepared to serve in Heaven if we do not serve here on earth. Acts 9:36-42 is the account of a very generous woman who served her Lord faithfully. Dorcas was a Jewess who lived among the Greeks. Her Hebrew name was Tabitha, but translated into Greek was Dorcas.[1] The English meaning of the name is *gazelle*. A gazelle is a slender, beautiful animal that is graceful and swift. Perhaps Dorcas was a beautiful woman; but whether beautiful or not, she was a woman full of good works.

Dorcas lived in Joppa which was a seaport on the Mediterranean Sea about thirty miles from Jerusalem. In this city lived many widows who had lost their husbands in shipwrecks. When they lost their husbands, they also lost their income. Again, there was no Social Security program in those days because God had instructed His people to care for widows and orphans.

22. What do these verses instruct regarding widows and orphans?

Exodus 22:22-24 _____

_____

Deuteronomy 10:17, 18 _____

_____

Deuteronomy 14:28, 29 _____

_____

Deuteronomy 24:19 _____

_____

23. Isaiah 54:4 and 5 give what comfort to a widow? _____

_____

Dorcas may have felt that she was not as gifted as other women that had preceded her. She was not a prophetess like Miriam or Deborah; neither was she a wife nor a mother. However, Scripture states that she was a disciple. A disciple is a follower of Christ. Dorcas had the faith of a Christian and that made all the difference. Faith is more than fellowship with God; one uses it to serve others also. True faith expresses itself in deeds.

24. What does James 2:26 tell us? _____

_____

Dorcas is also described as being "full of good works and almsdeeds which she did." This expresses her works of faith and her treatment of the sick, the poor, the widows and the orphans. She was an angel of mercy in the city of Joppa. Dorcas found her mission field at her doorstep. She was alert to the opportunities that were around her.

25. Name several opportunities for service you have available in your community (shut-ins, child evangelism, etc.). _____

_____

Dorcas was a woman whose deeds displayed her love. She would go into a home to help in time of sickness. She would do for a family what a mother normally would do. She visited the lonely. Because she was single and alone, she could identify with the women and therefore support them spiritually and morally. In this way, she utilized her full potential.

26. What was the special talent Dorcas used as a gift of serving (Acts 9:39)? _____

Because a woman is faithful to minister to others does not mean she will be free from the trials of life. One day Dorcas became ill. The nature of the illness is not told, but in time Dorcas died. Her home-going was a triumph for her labors and may have been acknowledged by her Lord, saying, "Inasmuch as ye have done it unto the least of these, my brethren, ye have done it unto me." However, her death was a heartbreak to her friends. The widows and orphans and overloaded mothers felt helpless—like sheep without a shepherd.

When Dorcas died, the people sent for the apostle Peter who was in a nearby town. Because Dorcas was a disciple of Jesus, the people believed they could get help from someone else who associated with Jesus. The people had heard of Peter's supernatural power (Acts 3:1-10; 5:15), and they felt sure he would come to their aid. Peter did arrive in Joppa and he did what he had seen the Lord do in a similar situation (Mark 5:40-42). He asked the people to leave the room and then he prayed and restored Dorcas to life through the power of God. Dorcas was one of seven people raised from the dead according to the Bible record. She was the only adult woman among that number.

The resurrection of Dorcas demonstrated the power of God in a remarkable way. The people realized God had performed the miracle, so they honored God rather than Peter or Dorcas. It was an act of mercy on the part of God and the outcome was that faith and joy were established in the entire city. Because of this miracle, "many believed on the Lord." The life, death and resurrection of Dorcas helped spread the gospel. Peter could not leave Joppa right away because he was needed by the people who were inquiring about God.

Dorcas started a movement that has spread all over the world. Today there are Dorcas Societies in almost every country. Millions of needy people are fed and clothed by this society.

Think of what godly women can do by way of service if they follow the example of Dorcas. They can give themselves to good works in the church by sewing, by nursing, by visiting the elderly, and by helping families in times of illness or death. These labors of love will be recognized as valuable by God as well as by men.

27. What is our admonition in James 1:27? _____

_____

Again, the Proverbs lady, like Dorcas, is a pattern for women. Both women do not merely throw a gift to those in need, but they extend warm sympathy and readiness to help those who are less fortunate by saying, "Place your confidence in me; I will do whatever I can; here, you have my hand."

PERSONAL APPLICATION

1. Ask the Lord to help you to be sensitive to the needs of others.

2. If you are single, 1 Corinthians 7:34 says, "The unmarried woman careth for the things of the Lord, that she may be holy both in body and in spirit. . . ." The unmarried woman is able to concentrate on the things of God. Without distraction she may give herself over to being "holy both in body and in spirit." "Holy" refers to her consecration that is unmodified by an earthly commitment. In contrast, the married woman must take into account the needs of her husband.

3. In love, serve others because "There is joy, joy, joy in serving Jesus." J-O-Y—Joy—is, "Jesus first, Yourself last and Others in-between."

4. Read *Improving Your Serve, The Art of Unselfish Living* by Charles Swindoll.

Using Your Gifts to Serve Others

O · Opportunity   *Whatsoever thy hand findeth to do, do it with thy might (Eccles. 9:10).*
T · Tears
H · Helpful
E · Enthusiastic   *And whatsoever ye do, do it heartily, as to the Lord, and not unto men (Col. 3:23).*
R · Ready
S · Sincere

1. Provide flowers for church services.
2. Baby-sit in pew for children of church musicians.
3. Clean artificial greenery.
4. Help in baptismal dressing room.
5. Be alert to needs of the pastor's family.
6. With your pastor's advice, develop a church library or cassette tape library.
7. Repair hymnbooks.
8. Help keep kitchen clean and supplied as well as cleaning other parts of the church; polish piano or pews.
9. Keep curtains clean and repaired.
10. Do art work: make posters, visual aids, bulletin boards.
11. Teach a class of girls or ladies in Sunday School, VBS, AWANA, Joy Club or be a camp counselor.
12. Help with mailings, typing, filing, sorting, answering mail.
13. Be a departmental secretary.
14. Help serve funeral dinners or assist with banquets.
15. Keep a scrapbook and pictures of church events.
16. Remember servicemen and college students with "goodies" and letters.
17. Correspond with church missionaries; provide a missionary cupboard.
18. Be a nursery helper, launder sheets, wash toys.
19. Work with children's church, junior choir.
20. Be a lobby greeter.
21. Volunteer to baby-sit for children of the pastor or Sunday School teachers.
22. Play a musical instrument or sing, join the choir, teach music.
23. Provide a clothing room and food pantry for needy families.
24. Visitation: soul winning, hospital, newcomers, canvassing, absentees.
25. Pray daily for the ministry of your church, pastor, deacons, teachers.
26. Practice hospitality: open home to missionaries, widows, singles.
27. "Adopt" a grandparent; minister to shut-ins and elderly; take in a meal.
28. Drive for a teen activity or be a chaperone.

29. Clean house for elderly or ill.
30. Don't neglect your family!

Be willing to serve others, but have the right attitude and motivation in doing so. Give yourself to some ministry—be busy doing what God wants you to do, and honor Him through your ministry.

"Others, Lord, yes others; Let me live for others, that I might live for Thee."

> **J** - Jesus
> **O** - Others
> **Y** - Yourself

NOTES

1. Harold Ockenga, *Women Who Made Bible History* (Grand Rapids: Zondervan Publishing House, 1962), 221.

Lesson 7

PATTERN FOR PREPAREDNESS

She is not afraid of the snow for her household: for all her household are clothed with scarlet. She maketh herself coverings of tapestry; her clothing is silk and purple (Proverbs 31:21, 22).

THE PROVERBS LADY is not afraid of the snow and cold weather. She knows the winds of winter will blow and howl and God will cover the earth with a blanket of snow, but she and her family are prepared.

Notice sometime how ants busy themselves all day in the summer "stockpiling" for the winter months ahead. Prepared women will do as the ant. Raising a garden in the summer is one way to be prepared for the winter. These frozen, dried or canned vegetables and fruits can be stored away for winter and will bring warm sunshine on a cold and cloudy day. Take time to bake extra cookies, cakes and casseroles and freeze them to be prepared for unexpected company that might drop by or for someone who becomes ill and needs them.

Ella May Miller in her book *The Joy of Housekeeping* offers some helpful hints regarding food preservation. Mrs. Miller quotes Dr. Don Paarlberg, top economist for the U. S. Department of Agriculture, as predicting an "increased price in processed fruits and vegetables because of production costs."[1]

Many homemakers pay the high price for these foods while others are looking for a way to avoid high prices. Gardening of course is one way to achieve a "lower total food bill." Living in an apartment or in an area where climate conditions are not conducive to gardening is difficult; however, some tomato plants will grow inside and bear delicious tomatoes. Sprouts can be grown in a pan in the window to garnish a salad. Perhaps the family would enjoy a drive to the country to buy fresh fruits and vegetables by the bushel. Many farm families are willing to share their produce if people are willing to pick the items they desire. Try sharing a garden spot with a friend to cut down on expenses, and have a good time of fellowship together hoeing and caring for the garden as "many hands make light work."

After securing the fresh fruits and vegetables, prepare them immediately to avoid spoilage. Prompt and careful handling means much in retaining fresh flavor, texture, and nutrient value. Buy or plant only the foods the family will eat.

The preparation for freezing vegetables consists of washing them, cutting them into desired lengths, blanching them for about three minutes in boiling water and draining and cooling them thoroughly. Place them in an air tight container allowing one-half inch at the top for expansion.

To freeze fruit, wash it, cut in desired pieces, place in containers, add sugar (if desired) and seal. Various sizes of jars can be used; just remember to let them thaw at room temperature.

Some homemakers prefer to can fruits and vegetables. If this is the case, you will need a pressure cooker accompanied with detailed instructions.

When canning and freezing it is good to consult with the local home economist through the state Extension Service for the best techniques and methods.

A woman's creativity is expressed when she prepares for the winter by "stockpiling" garden produce. The family has to eat, so she takes advantage of the opportunity to lower the food costs.

1. What advice is offered by Solomon in Proverbs 12:11? ___

Notice that not only does the Proverbs lady have her pantry full and is prepared for fixing nutritious meals, but she has taken the time to sew warm clothing for her family to prepare them for winter storms, *"for all her household are clothed with scarlet."* Dr. Ironside states, "Some prefer 'scarlet' to be translated 'double garments' as they do not see what the color has to do with keeping out the cold; but the word is never so translated elsewhere in Scripture. It is the scarlet obtained from the Tola, a cochineal-like insect, which, being crushed, produces a fine red, or rich crimson dye. It is the 'worm' of Psalm 22:6, to which our Lord likens Himself. He was bruised and slain that all His redeemed might be clothed in splendor for eternity."[2] Matthew Henry suggests that "double garments" may refer to having a "change of raiment, a winter suit and a summer suit." The color scarlet or red will hold heat in comparison to white garments which keep out the heat. Wool also preserves warmth; therefore, the Proverbs lady makes red woolen garments for her family to wear in the winter's cold. These "red flannels" are made in the summertime and are ready and waiting for winter wear.

"She maketh herself coverings of tapestry; her clothing is silk and purple." In this 22nd verse, the Proverbs woman is doing upholstery work. This is in reference to pillows or mattresses. She makes soft feather beds with covers, cushions and rugs.

Her own clothing is rich and fine, it is silk and purple. The silk in this passage is a fine, white linen, glistening like silk, as the bride arrayed in Revelation 19. In other places in Scripture, purple and linen are used together as the attire of the well-clothed (Luke 16:19). Though she is not so vain as to spend a great deal of time dressing herself, yet she has rich clothes and wears them well. The robes her husband wears are of her spinning also, and they look better and wear better than any that are purchased.

The purple is obtained from the juice of a certain species of shellfish found on the eastern shores of the Mediterranean Sea. The juice of the entire fish is not used, just a little bit of liquid contained in a vessel in the neck.

The Proverbs woman is always in style because she sews her wardrobe. She is fashionable and looks nice because she always wants to remain attractive to her husband. When he comes home from work, she has on a fresh outfit, just the right amount of makeup and looks like she has just started her day rather than being on the verge of collapsing. She has even made herself some silk negligees, her husband's favorite kind.

Suppose a woman does not know how to sew? She can learn. The money invested in a sewing machine will more than pay for itself if it is put to good use. Perhaps she could start out with a good used machine or borrow her mother's or a friend's until she gets the feel of sewing, then invest in a model of sewing machine that would best fit her needs. After obtaining a machine, get a sewing tray or box. Keeping sewing items in order is rule number one. Some basic equipment to purchase before beginning to sew is: straight pins, sewing needles, thread, shears, tape measure, seam ripper, tailor's chalk and a hem gauge. Keep the iron and ironing board close at hand also.

Next, select a pattern. It is wise for the beginning seamstress to choose a simple pattern, one that takes a minimum amount of fitting and not much detail. Avoid a collar or set-in sleeves. A shift dress is a good pattern for a beginner. The choice of material is also important. The easiest fabrics to work with are linen, cotton percale, wool flannel and polyester. Stripes and plaids should be avoided in the beginning stages of sewing.

Purchase a pattern before selecting the material. The pattern will indicate the amount of yardage and also suggest suitable materials out of which the garment can be made. Pattern sizes are not always the same as ready-to-wear sizes; therefore, a woman should know her measurements. She should look for the closest measurements to hers on the pattern guide.

Some pattern companies advertise that a lady can make an outfit tonight and wear it tomorrow. To do so is faster and easier than shopping when she cannot find the color or style she is looking for in the dress shops. The bonus is the money she saves by sewing her own clothes.

There is instant tea, instant coffee and instant potatoes. A beginning seamstress may want to purchase a copy of *Instant Sewing,* published by Graphic Enterprises, Inc. This small book can be purchased at a fabric store or ordered from Box 155, Old Chelsea Station, Department R3, New York, New York, 10011, for $1.00. The following are some of the tips offered from the book on how to make the distinction between "homemade" and "couture."

Press as you work.

Follow steps given in the pattern instruction sheet.

Fit garment carefully before final stitching.

Use sewing aids: buttonhole makers, button covering kits, belt and buckle kits.

Use a magnet seam guide or contact tape on the machine to help you sew even seams.

Let a bias cut garment hang a few days before marking the hem.

By designing her own garments, a woman can correct figure faults (most ladies have some): broad shoulders, narrow shoulders, broad hips and heavy thighs, too long waisted or high waisted, wanting to look "pounds thinner" or gain a few pounds.

With unlimited funds, a woman could hire a name designer to do her yearly wardrobe. With limited funds and a bit of creativity, she can achieve the same effect—and earn the satisfaction that goes with it.

The Christian woman is careful of her own appearance. She must keep her body and clothes clean. She does not need to dress expensively—she can watch for sales on material and clothing so that she does not spend more money than is budgeted.

From verses 21 and 22, it is obvious that the Proverbs woman is prepared for living, but she is also prepared for dying because she knows the Savior.

2. What is the admonition of Amos 4:12? _____

_____

3. What do the following verses tell us?

Isaiah 43:2 _____

Hebrews 9:27 _____

No matter how well prepared a person is to face death and dying, it catches them at the worst possible moment.

4. The Psalmist wrote some remarkable words about the lifestyle he desired. What does he say in the following verses?

Psalm 17:15 _____

Psalm 39:4 _____

Psalm 90:5 _____

Psalm 90:6 _____

Psalm 90:10 _____

Psalm 90:12 _____

Look at another Bible woman who was prepared to die to save her people, and as a result, her courage saved a nation. Plan about one-half hour this week to read the entire book of Esther, noting particularly 4:1-5, 7:1-6 and 8:15-17. Following is the account of Esther taken from *The Bible in Verse* by Alvy E. Ford.[3]

Esther

Chapter 1
Persia's great king sends for
Vashti, his queen.
She is reluctant to come and
be seen.
Thus she arouses his majesty's
hate.
Then she is cast from her royal
estate.

Chapter 2
Esther, a Jewess, is chosen as
queen,
Being the fairest of all to be
seen.
Mordecai learns of a plot toward
the king,
Promptly tells Esther, exposing
the thing.

Chapter 3
Haman is raised to a lofty estate.
He for the Jews has a terrible
hate.
Mordecai dares to refuse him
his dues.
Haman then plots to destroy
all the Jews.

Chapter 4
Now do the Jews go to fasting
and prayer.
Esther might help their calamity spare.
Mordecai sends her an urgent
behest.
Esther prepares to present her
request.

Chapter 5
Esther goes forth; her reception
is fine.
Then she bids husband and
Haman to dine.
Haman exults in his swaggering
way,
Plans to have Mordecai hanged
the next day.

Chapter 6
Haman is humbled, receiving
a blow,
Being compelled now to honor
his foe.
Mordecai rides in a kingly
estate.
Haman is grieved at his own
crushing fate.

Chapter 7
Esther now offers the banquet
prepared,
Brings her request that her
people be spared.
King is enraged at what Haman
has done.
Haman is hanged, and reprieve
is begun.

Chapter 8
Mordecai climbs to a lofty
estate.
Esther beseeches the king for
her fate.
King may not alter his former
decree.
Jews are permitted to fight to
be free.

Chapter 9

Now the great day of the battle
 arrives:
Heathen are slaughtered but
 Israel thrives.
Thus shall these days be
 remembered with cheer;
Two days of Purim are honored
 each year.

Chapter 10

Mordecai really is great in the
 land,
Standing right next to the king
 in command;
Being accepted by all of the
 Jews,
Seeking their very best welfare
 to choose.

The story of Esther has the atmosphere of the Cinderella story mixed with the scorching smell of Hitler's gas chambers. Even though the name of God does not appear once in the original Hebrew, His presence is evident on every page.

Esther may have started the first beauty contest on record. One may admire a beautiful landscape or a well-formed horse or a strong man, but there is nothing that excites admiration like a beautiful woman.

5. What kind of woman was Esther (2:2, 3, 7)? _____

_____

6. Besides being beautiful, Esther was also obedient to her cousin named _____ (2:5, 7), who treated her as his own daughter.

7. How was King Ahasuerus impressed with Esther (2:17)?

_____

8. What was recorded in the book of the chronicles (2:21-23)? _____

_____

"Mordecai, who served the royal court, was hated by the king's chancellor, Haman, an Amalekite. Haman was brilliant, ambitious and rude. He spared no one. However, the king respected him highly and ordered all servants at the royal court to bow down before him. Mordecai was the only person who refused. Because he was a Jew, the only person he would bow before was God. Haman was so embittered by this rejection that he decided to kill Mordecai and all other Jews in the Persian empire.

"He conceived a scheme so subtle that no Jew would be able to escape. All would be caught in the trap Haman was setting. The total annihilation of the Jews—God's people—was announced. The king's signature made it possible for Haman to wipe them off the globe forever. Royal couriers took the fastest animals and rushed to every corner of the immense empire to announce the coming calamity. The Jews were appalled and terrified.

"Esther had been married for five years. At the request of Mordecai, she remained silent about her Jewish heritage, but he kept her informed daily on the situation. With the grim extinction of the Jews in sight, Mordecai felt that the only solution was for Esther to intervene."[4]

9. What did Mordecai advise Esther to ask the king (4:8)?

_____

"Her people" meant she must reveal her Jewish origin, which she had not done. Now Mordecai says she must tell the king and ask his help to save her people. How would the king react? Would he feel she had deceived him? Perhaps he hated her race as much as Haman and many others.

10. What was another obstacle Esther faced (4:11)? _____

_____

No one was allowed to present himself to the king without being summoned, not even the queen. Since the king had not called Esther to come to him for thirty days, she had no guarantee that he loved her as before.

11. What was Mordecai's reply to Esther (4:13, 14)? _____

"From another place . . ." Mordecai was thinking about God. God would not allow Haman to murder the Jewish nation. Throughout the ages God had promised the Messiah would come through this people. Haman could not prevent this. Neither could Satan. Though the need for deliverance was immediate, Mordecai's trust in God was solid.

Esther had an attitude of dependence upon God. She commanded Mordecai, "Gather together all the Jews . . . and fast ye for me. . . ." This fasting was for the purpose of praying. She realized she was a powerless woman and her help could come only from the God of Israel. She prayed for three days and three nights, realizing her need for God's guidance because she needed wisdom and courage to act properly.

12. What was Esther's decision (4:16)? _____

13. Summarize 5:1-8. _____

_____

_____

14. In chapter 6, the king cannot sleep. What important facts were read to him? _____

15. Because Mordecai had saved the king's life, what did the king do (6:6-11)? _____

_____

"Through Esther's intercession, Ahasuerus condemned Haman to death and passed the decree that the Jews were permitted to defend themselves on the day on which Haman had decreed their extermination. Thus, the 13th and 14th of Nisan was set aside as a celebration of the Jews which is observed today, called the Feast of Purim, to celebrate the deliverance under Esther."[5]

Esther paved the way, unknown to her, for the coming of Christ. Through her, God has also indicated that His guidance is available to His followers for making decisions in life.

16. Gien Karssen in *Her Name Is Woman*[6] lists some ways to test our decisions:

Based on the Word of God (John 14:21) _____

_____

Seek God's wisdom (James 1:5) _____

_____

Counsel from others (Prov. 15:22) _____

_____

Inner peace (1 John 3:21) _____

_____

God-opened doors (Rev. 3:7, 8) _____

_____

Through Esther and the Proverbs woman, women today can have the assurance that God is still guiding His people; therefore, women can be prepared for life as well as for death by having a personal relationship with God through Jesus Christ.

PERSONAL APPLICATION

1. Purchase a copy of *The Joy of Housekeeping* by Ella May Miller. This book contains helpful advice regarding many facets of being a prepared homemaker.

2. Do some gardening and then can, freeze or dry your produce. *Blue Book* by Ball is an easy guide to canning and freezing.

3. Exchange patterns with a same-sized friend. This will add variety to your wardrobe without investing in more patterns.

4. Seek God's guidance daily in your life as you serve Him. Ask Him to help you be prepared for any situation that may arise in your life.

NOTES

1. Miller, *The Joy of Housekeeping,* 65.
2. Ironside, *Notes on the Book of Proverbs,* 478.
3. Alvy E. Ford, *The Bible in Verse* (Lincoln, NE: Back to the Bible Publishers, 1955), 98-100.
4. Gien Karssen, *Her Name Is Woman* (Colorado Springs, CO: Nav-Press, 1975), 115, 116.
5. Ockenga, *Women Who Made Bible History,* 155.
6. Karssen, 116.

Lesson 8

PATTERN FOR PRUDENCE

She openeth her mouth with wisdom; and in her tongue is the law of kindness. She looketh well to the ways of her household, and eateth not the bread of idleness (Proverbs 31:26, 27).

TO BE PRUDENT IS to be "cautious in conduct; wise; not rash; exercising sound judgment; circumspect." The Proverbs lady is prudent as she opens her mouth with skillful and godly wisdom. Wisdom in this passage of Proverbs is divine wisdom, the application of Biblical knowledge to everyday life. When this lady speaks, it is God's wisdom.

1. Define God's wisdom according to James 3:17. _____

_____

2. What is the beginning of wisdom (Prov. 9:10)? _____

_____

3. Where do we find wisdom (James 1:5)? _____

_____

Read the account of Solomon's dream in 1 Kings 3:5-15. Ladies today have just as much right as Solomon to request wisdom. They must realize that with this precious gift comes a great responsibility—they must act on what they now understand.

4. How do we profit from gaining wisdom (Prov. 3:13-15)?

_____

_____

5. What are the attributes of wisdom (Prov. 8:12-20)? _____

_____

There is no bitter envying, jealousy or strife in the heart of the Proverbs woman (James 3:14, 15). What she knows of divine wisdom she uses wisely, so that she becomes a blessing and benefit to others. She is discreet and firm, yet very kind. Therefore, others seek her prudent advice and confide in her because she never gossips.

The reputation of many has been ruined to the gossiper's tune of "have you heard." A good policy to follow is this: know gossip is true before repeating it, and then do not repeat it!

Spoken words are never forgotten. The Bible makes some penetrating statements on the subject of the tongue.

6. What are these statements regarding the tongue?

Psalm 35:28 _____

Psalm 51:14 _____

Psalm 71:24 _____

Psalm 126:2 _____

Psalm 139:4 _____

Proverbs 15:4

Proverbs 21:23 _____

James 1:26 _____

James 3:5, 6 _____

When a woman invites Christ into her life, **the first member of her body to be under the Holy Spirit's control should be her tongue.** She must become increasingly aware of what she says. As she hears her own words in conversation, they must be pleasing to God.

7. How does James describe the tongue in James 3:8? _____

_____

The New American Standard Bible translates Proverbs 31:26, *"the teaching of kindness is on her tongue,"* referring to the instruction the Proverbs woman gives to others. By the words of her mouth she urges consideration, love, aid, sympathy and courtesy. Instead of petty complaints and slanderous stories, her lips pour forth words of loving-kindness to hearers who are edified and refreshed (Prov. 10:31).

The King James Version of the Bible reads, *"in her tongue is the law of kindness"* (Prov. 31:26). This has to do with self-imposed restrictions on her own speech. A law is a regulation by God or by the government under which one is to live. The pattern woman has put herself under legal restrictions that she speaks only in kindness. She has made kindness a law of life. Because of the pureness of her heart, her tongue delights to utter words of grace and truth in steadfast love.

8. How does this contrast with the angry and contentious woman in these verses?

Proverbs 21:19 _____

Proverbs 27:15 _____

9. What is Paul's statement in Ephesians 4:31, 32? _____

_____

When a woman lets her tongue speak in an unchristian pattern, she breaks this law of kindness. This is as much of a sin in God's eyes as murder or adultery. Sin is lawlessness or any violation of God's laws or His standards.

10. A daily guide for conversation should be

Psalm 19:14 _____

Psalm 141:3 _____

An eminent French political writer states, "The greatest problem in life is the pain we cause in the lives of others. Some of this pain is caused intentionally, and springs from hearts of stone; but by far the largest amount is given without active intention or premeditated plan. Selfishness, which blinds us to the peculiarities of others, ignorance, stupidity, thoughtlessness, unnecessary criticism, uncalled-for advice, course witticism and a thousand other agencies are the means of wounding feelings, hurting sensibilities, stinging pride, dampening the ardor and quenching the effort of fellow men and women, and striking the keenest pain into hearts which will never cease to quiver from it."

The following article, "The Stoning" by Marjorie Holmes, demonstrates what can often happen in conversation:

> Lord, I detest myself right now. I've just come from a luncheon where four of us spent most of our time criticizing a mutual friend. We discussed her eccentricities, how extravagant and undependable she is, how she spoils her children, her vanity and how eager she always is to be attractive to men.
>
> While a lot of these things are true, Lord—they really are—even as I joined in I found myself wondering: Who are we to judge? Did it make us feel better about ourselves to brandish the defects of somebody so much 'worse'?
>
> Well, I don't feel better about myself now. I keep thinking of what Jesus said to the men about to stone the adulterous woman: 'Which of you is without sin?' Yet there we sat, self-righteously stoning our sister with words.
>
> How, Lord, can I make amends? I long to call her up and beg her forgiveness, but that would be a terrible mistake. She would be so hurt, so much damage would be done. No, all I can do is to ask Your forgiveness. And pray for her. Help her, strengthen her, bless her. Don't let her ever know what we said about her, please.
>
> And oh, Lord, put more compassion in my heart, guard my tongue. Don't let me ever again join in stoning a sister— or anyone else—with words.[1]

It has been said that people possess what they confess. If someone constantly has negative thoughts and talks about depression and sickness, they either possess those things or those things possess the person.

11. What does Proverbs 23:7 tell us? _____

_____

12. What did Jesus say in Matthew 12:34-37? _____

_____

The Bible teaches that words carry everlasting consequences. By yielding to the Holy Spirit within, love becomes the source of the words which flow from lips into the listening ears of family, friends, fellow Christians and the world.

Ladies must be careful when sharing prayer burdens that "sharing" does not develop into gossip concerning the needs of others. Spiritual discernment must be used in this area.

13. Proverbs 11:13 has good advice regarding this matter.

_____

14. Advice is also given in

Proverbs 15:1 _____

Colossians 4:6 _____

15. What does Paul admonish in Ephesians 4:23-25? _____

_____

Each Christian is a member of the Body of Jesus Christ and belongs to Him. Christians are also members of one another, as the fingers are of the hand, and the hand of the arm. Christians need to minister to each other by loving, encouraging and praying for one another. One day they will be presented as the Bride of Christ, without spot or wrinkle (Eph. 5:27). Instead of criticizing the spots and wrinkles, Christians should smooth out the wrinkles and remove the spots whenever and wherever they can.

16. What else does Paul say in Ephesians 4:29? _____

_____

The kind of woman God wants is one whose words refresh and are a blessing to others. She should have a gracious and positive attitude that uplifts and encourages others.

Nothing goes on in the household of the Proverbs lady that escapes her observation because *"she looketh well to the ways of her household." "Looketh"* means to keep the watch (guard duty); she continually watches with a keen eye the direction her family is headed. She notices the habits, actions and speech of her children. She exercises firm but loving discipline over each child and offers encouragement to each when it is needed. It means knowing where each family member is, who he is with, how he is progressing in school or at his job, and what his hopes and dreams are. It means taking time to listen to each one in her household, letting them know she loves them. She also makes sure her family has the proper food and nutrition, fun and relaxation.

Even though the man is to be the spiritual leader of the family, a woman can be "on guard" in the area of spiritual development. She should know where each member of the household is in his relationship to God. This can be done not only by conversation but also by observation. Does the teenager's Bible gather dust from Sunday to Sunday? Does the eight-year-old talk about becoming a missionary when he grows up? If the child should say, "Mommy, I want to ask Jesus into my heart. What should I do?" a mother should be able to present God's plan of salvation to her child.

Meeting the needs in the household requires a great deal of planning and thought. While doing some mentally untaxing jobs such as making beds, folding the laundry or doing the dishes, a woman can prayerfully consider the methods of meeting each person's needs. By doing this, she is taking pains in the duty of her place and also takes pleasure in doing it.

One reason the Proverbs lady is able to keep watch over the doings and goings of her household is because she does not eat the bread of idleness or sluggishness. She knows that no one was sent into this world to be idle. When women have nothing to do, the devil will soon find something for them to do—idle hands are the devil's workshop. This idleness may result in gossip, discontent or self-pity (1 Tim. 5:13).

One of the easiest traps of idlenesss for women at home during the day is television. The hours wasted by Christians watching soap operas is beyond computation. Occasionally soap operas have been blamed for a divorce because the wife watched television all day, ignoring her husband, her children and her home. The television characters became more real to her than her own family.

The great danger of these soap operas is the life-style they portray which is contrary to the Christian pattern of life. Consider the following:

Alice falls in love with Steve. They plan to marry. Alice discovers that Steve has had an affair with Rachel who just happens to be married to Alice's brother Russ. It's a toss-up who fathered Rachel's baby. After much mental trauma, true love triumphs and Alice and Steve wed. But Alice catches an innocent Steve in a compromising situation with Rachel. Divorce. Steve woos Alice again. Remarriage. Meanwhile, Russ is shed of Rachel, and she is having a great time running wild, giving everybody grief. And Alice's other sister, Pat, is having her problems too. Her husband, John, was Pat's lawyer when Pat was accused of murdering her boyfriend after he talked her into an abortion after he got her pregnant out of wedlock. John got Pat off and married her. Short-lived bliss. John has an accident and is crippled for a couple of whiny years. Recovery. Pat has no children. Anguish. Corrective surgery, twins who grow to be teen-agers in about three years. John has an affair. . . .[2]

Add to this the various murders, affairs, slanders, drug and alcohol addictions, and general "hanky-panky" on the part of the rest of the characters—what a way of life. Certainly it is not what Christ would admonish.

Not only can soap operas stain a woman's mind, but unpure books can also captivate her fantasy.

17. What are Christian's instructed to do in Philippians 4:8?

_____

_____

18. Paul has further advice in 2 Corinthians 10:5. _____

_____

19. What are other Bible verses that deal with our thoughts?

Job 21:27 _____

Job 42:2 _____

Psalm 94:11 _____

Proverbs 12:5 _____

Proverbs 15:26 _____

Isaiah 55:8, 9 _____

It is necessary for a woman to be prudent as she keeps a watch over her life so she may live a life that is pleasing unto the Lord.

20. To avoid the snares of the world, we must **watch** our

W - Words (Matt. 12:36) _____

A - Actions (Phil. 1:27) _____

T - Thoughts (Prov. 23:7) _____

C - Companions (Prov. 13:20) _____

H - Home (Deut. 6:4-9) _____

PERSONAL APPLICATION

1. Ask the Lord to make your ears sensitive to your own words, that they will glorify Him and bring blessings to others.

2. Seek the Lord's guidance as you look to the ways of your household, that He will give you the wisdom that you need (James 1:5).

3. "Keep your words soft and sweet; you never know which ones you will have to eat."

4. Principles to practice from Proverbs for good Christian conversation:

Always speak the truth (Prov. 6:16, 17, 19).
Speak few words, speak wisely (Prov. 10:19; 17:27; 29:11).
Good words can make people feel better (Prov. 12:18, 25; 15:30; 16:24).
Stop quarrels with soft words (Prov. 15:1).
Think before you speak (Prov. 15:28; 18:13, 17; 20:25; 29:20).
Proper and fitting words are beautiful (Prov. 25:11).
Soft speech is powerful (Prov. 25:15).
Speak out for justice (Prov. 31:8, 9).

5. Speech Habits Quiz from Proverbs 10:18-21:

Do you use words sparingly (10:19)? _____

Are your words worth listening to (10:20)? _____

Do your words nourish and instruct others (10:21)? _____
(If you answered "no" to one or more, chances are your speech habits could use an overhaul.)

6. Write out and memorize these verses:

Psalm 19:14 _____

Psalm 139:4 _____

Psalm 141:3 _____

Philippians 1:27 _____

STOP! LOOK! LISTEN!

(Guidelines for music, movies, books, television)

1. *Does it have curse words?* These days it's difficult to escape

from hearing or reading curse words. "Damn" has become an ordinary everyday word; however, God is the only One Who has the right to use that word and the only One Who is in the damning business. We often use the word "darn" which is only an abbreviated form of damn.

2. *Does it have words or phrases that put down God, parents or authority?* God put parents in every home as a representative of God's authority. Anything that puts down marriage or authority ought to be put down in your life. Some people are anti-authoritarian in their philosophy and do not realize how ungodly this is. Read Romans 13 and Hebrews 13.

3. *Does it have words and phrases that promote sexual thoughts?* If you are unmarried and listening, watching or reading something that promotes, encourages and stimulates emotions of sexual desires,—"put it on the shelf." Be careful of mixing romantic music and sensual words.

4. *Does the beat make you feel fleshly and wild?* A beat that makes you feel fleshly and wild is wrong. King Saul had David play because he wanted his spirits lifted. He was in a bad, foul mood. There are many songs and programs that lift your spirits, but don't let them lift the spirits toward the flesh. Actually, they can lower your spirits.

5. *Does it take you toward Jesus?* Anything that would turn us away from Christ and His attributes is wrong.

6. *Is it the type of thing you listen to when you feel like backsliding?* Everyone feels like backsliding once in a while. When you say, "I want to kick up my heels a little bit; I'm just going to get with it and have some fun," be careful! If it's the sort of thing that makes you feel like backsliding even a little bit, you should eliminate it from your life.

7. *Are you cautious about singers, actors, authors and what you know about their lives?* Often these people do not practice what they preach.

> *I beseech you therefore, brethren, by the mercies of God, that ye present [yield] your bodies a living sacrifice, holy, acceptable unto God, which is your reasonable service (Rom. 12:1).*
>
> *Finally, brethren, whatsoever things are true, whatsoever things are honest, whatsoever things are just, whatsoever things*

are pure, whatsoever things are lovely, whatsoever things are of good report; if there be any virtue, and if there be any praise, think on these things (Phil. 4:8).

We have a hard job to do: To be *in* the world and not *of* the world!

NOTES

1. Marjorie Holmes Mighell, *Hold Me Up a Little Longer, Lord* (Double-day and Co., Inc., 1977). Printed in *Woman's Day*, (November, 1977).

2. Roper, *Wife, Mate, Mother, Me!* 84.

Lesson 9

PATTERN FOR LOVE

Her children arise up, and call her blessed; her husband also, and he praiseth her. Many daughters have done virtuously, but thou excellest them all (Proverbs 31:28, 29).

DO NOT BE SURPRISED to find that everyone loves this Proverbs woman. She is lovable and she lives a consistent life as wife and mother; therefore, it is easy for her husband and children to love, honor, respect and praise her. She is a great blessing to her family. She expresses constant love and care to her children. Each morning as they awake and smell breakfast, they think of their mother and how she cares for them. Her husband praises her too. Though busy with her projects of sewing and gardening and caring for the household, she makes time for her husband so they can develop their relationship. Like Ruth, her neighbors also praise her for the whole town knows she is a virtuous woman (Ruth 3:11).

The husband in Proverbs compares his wife to *"many daughters"* when he tells her she excels them all. This is quite a compliment, considering the daughters of Jewish history—Sarah, Rebekah, Rachel, Ruth, Naomi, Hannah and countless others. What a tribute to be compared favorably with these great women.

Everyone appreciates compliments. They prove that others recognize an individual's value; they are evidences of love, affection and friendship. Everyone should be praised when they deserve it.

Parents should be teaching their children the value of compliments, and they should do it by setting a good example of praise in action.

Praise is meant to be received, yet how many times has someone brushed aside a compliment as flattery or almost as a lie? This kind of behavior is basically rude because it makes the giver of the compliment feel foolish.

Suppose a man tells a woman, "You look lovely" and her reply is, "Oh, you don't mean that. You're just saying it." In effect, she is calling him a liar. A woman must be careful about this. A man who is hurt because she has forgotten the law of kindness will be reluctant to offer her compliments again.

The Psalms are full of compliments and praise to God.

1. What does Psalm 106.1, 2 say? _____

_____

Of course, compliments are one way of demonstrating love.

2. What does 1 Corinthians 13:13 tell us? _____

_____

"Love" is one of the most overused yet undervalued words in the English language. People "love" anything ranging from food to pets, a child or God. However, the Greeks had four words denoting love. *Stergo* is the word for love that describes natural affection, contentment or satisfaction. This is a feeling of security in the relationship between two people. A second kind of love is *eros* or the love of passion which draws two marriage partners together into an intimate relationship. *Phileo* is a third kind of love, a friendly or brotherly love based on mutual attraction; the type of love experienced for fellow Christians. The fourth kind of love is *agape,* a self-sacrificing love. It is the love that will cause a wife to sacrifice herself and her wishes in the interest of the well-being of her husband. This *agape* love is the word used in John 3:16, expressing "For God so loved the world, that He gave His only begotten Son."

The two "love chapters" in the New Testament are 1 John 4 and 1 Corinthians 13.

3. Why is love expected of a Christian (1 John 4:7)? _____

_____

4. What are Christians admonished to do in 1 John 4:11?

_____

5. Why do Christians love God (1 John 4:19)? _____

_____

6. Who is said to be a liar (1 John 4:20)? _____

_____

7. What commandment is stated in 1 John 4:21? _____

_____

Read 1 Corinthians 13. This passage is a spiritual clinic on love. The Greek word for love in this chapter is *agape*.

8. Name some things that are profitless without love (vv. 1-3).

_____

_____

_____

9. How will divine love show through in the life of a Christian (v. 4)? _____

10. What effect does this love have on outward manners (v. 5)?

_____

_____

Although "easily provoked" is not in the original Greek, it literally means "not exasperated"—love does not fly off the handle.

11. Can real love ever allow one to be glad when someone else does wrong (v. 6)? _____

12. In what ways does love rejoice (v. 6)? _____

13. List four ways love is manifested in verse 7:

_____

_____

14. _____ never fails (v. 8).

15. The highest affection of the soul is _____ (v. 13).

16. What is the first and great commandment (Matt. 22:37, 38)? _____

_____

A young lawyer asked Jesus, "Who is my neighbor?" and Jesus answered with the story of the Good Samaritan (Luke 10:30-37).

17. Based on the teaching in these verses in Luke, who is your neighbor? _____

18. What does Jesus say in John 13:34, 35? _____

_____

Jesus gave the world the right to judge Christians on the basis of their observable love for one another. The world can judge whether or not a person is truly born-again by the love he manifests for all other Christians. This demonstrated love is a testimony to the world of the Christian's discipleship. How true is the chorus, "And they will know we are Christians by our love." This is the Christian's testimony.

19. Love will cause us to be _____

_____ (Rom. 12:10).

20. Where divine love reigns, we will _____

_____ (Col. 3:13).

21. What is said of those who give no thought to individuals in need (1 John 3:17)? _____

22. Love implanted by the Holy Spirit can enable a Christian to _____

_____ (Luke 6:35).

23. Here are some ways to express love.

Notice people. Do not get so wrapped up in yourself you forget others. Notice when someone has a new dress or suit or a new hairdo.

Be considerate. When entertaining for company as well as your family, serve the foods they enjoy. Wives, know what outfit your husband likes and wear it often. Even when shopping for a new outfit, know his favorite colors and style so your wardrobe will please him.

Courtesy and politeness are a must. Saying "thank you" and "please" does not hurt anyone. The Bible says, "A word fitly spoken is like apples of gold in pictures of silver" (Prov. 25:11).

Do not be resentful. Ephesians 4:26, 27 says, "Be ye angry, and sin not: let not the sun go down upon your wrath: Neither give place to the devil." We all do some things that bother others; therefore, we need to find out what they are and get rid of them. Learn to talk things out and get them settled.

Cultivate common interests. Learn to be interested in the hobbies, sports and activities of others. A husband and wife particularly need to develop common interests other than the children so that when the "empty nest" days appear, they can have a bond of closeness even without the children around.

There are two kinds of love. There is the love by feeling that springs from the emotions and fluctuates with changing moods; and there is the love by willing in which one exercises the will to love. Women should be maturing in love each passing day as they develop their Christian walk, pressing toward the goal of being like Christ. They should seek to develop *agape* love, which is a self-denying compassion and has its source in God.

24. What does 1 Thessalonians 3:12, 13 tell us? _____ _____

_____

Love for God will be demonstrated by the place His commandments occupy in the Christian's life; therefore, it is necessary to study the Bible to learn what God's commandments are.

25. What did Jesus say in the following verses?

John 14:12 _____

John 14:15 _____

God made people to love and to be loved. To love is to really live, to experience the deepest kind of soul satisfaction.

26. What is the supreme evidence of God's boundless love (Rom. 5:8)? _____

A woman may feel she is loved according to her performance—if she does not perform acceptably, she is not loved as much. God's love is not based on performance. He loves unconditionally, whether a woman's performance is good or bad.

27. What do these verses verify regarding God's love for us?

Deuteronomy 7:7, 8 _____

_____

Jeremiah 31:3 _____

John 17:23 _____

Romans 8:35-39 _____

_____

Ephesians 3:17-19 _____

_____

Knowing that God loves unconditionally, a woman should have a proper and real love and acceptance of herself. This is not pride or selfishness—it is agreeing with God that her creation is good as He said in Genesis 1:31, "Behold, it was very good."

It is necessary that a woman have proper love for herself in order to have self-respect. Then she can recognize and accept her weaknesses and inabilities and feel comfortable, thus accepting herself and being at peace. She does not envy another's gifts, abilities or temperament. She is content with herself but also strives to be more and more like Jesus Christ. It is having a desire to grow but at the same time realizing she is already a person of worth and of value, acceptable and lovable.

Verse 29 of Proverbs 31 says, *"Many daughters have done virtuously, but thou excellest them all."* As mentioned at the beginning of this lesson, the husband in Proverbs speaks well of his wife as a virtuous woman. Virtue will have its praise (Phil. 4:8). Virtuous women are as rare and as precious as jewels according to

Proverbs 31:10. The virtuous woman excels all other women.

Proverbs 31:29 records a great deal about the Proverbs woman regarding her private life. It seems she has done more than Miriam, the leader of a nation's women, in praise to God (Exod. 15:20, 21); Deborah, the patriotic military advisor (Judg. 4:4-10); Huldah, the woman who revealed God's secret message to national leaders (2 Kings 22:14); Ruth, the woman of constancy (Ruth 1:16); Hannah, the ideal mother (1 Sam. 1:20; 2:19); and more than Queen Esther, the woman who risked sacrificing her life for her people (Esther 4:16).

What greater earthly happiness could this virtuous woman know than her children's reverence and her husband's blessing? Picture her crowned with years, her children grown up, perhaps themselves surrounded with families, and endeavoring to train their children as they themselves had been trained. Their mother is constantly before their eyes. Her tender guidance, her wise counsel, her loving discipline and her holy example are vividly kept in remembrance. They do not cease to *"call her blessed,"* and to thank the Lord for her, as His invaluable gift. Her husband praises her, not for deceitful and vain charms of beauty but because she has reverence for the Lord. Therefore, in his eyes she is his support in the declining years, the soother of his cares, the counsellor of his perplexities, the comforter of his sorrows, the sunshine of his earthly joys. Both children and husband combine in the grateful acknowledgement, *"Many daughters have done virtuously, but thou excellest them all."*

The Proverbs woman is able to excel because of her spiritual and practical devotion to God, which permeates every area and relationship of her life. All seven of the Christian virtues listed in 2 Peter 1:5-7 are demonstrated in her life like colored threads of tapestry. Read these verses.

From this passage in 2 Peter, believers are told that because of their salvation something else is expected. Based upon faith (salvation) believers are to be fully equipped with the seven virtues or graces listed in verses 5 through 7. The idea Peter expresses seems to be that as one virtue is exercised, the next is developed until the ultimate is reached. It may be illustrated in the following way as building blocks.

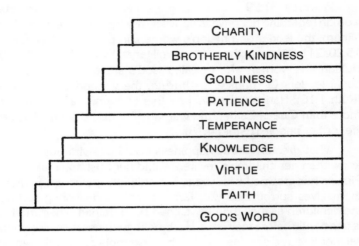

"The foundation of faith based on God's Word having been laid, the Christian must then move on to build up that transaction which has been completed. *'Virtue'* in this context probably means courage. Courage is needed not only because of the attack of Satan, but also because of his attractions. As courage is exercised, knowledge will grow. This may speak of the practical knowledge of what to do in particular situations. As knowledge is exercised, temperance will be increased. Temperance refers to self-control—the ability to get a grip on oneself. As temperance is exercised, patience will be evident. Many start out great, but they never last because of the temptation to become discouraged. As patience is exercised, godliness will characterize the Christian. Godliness is seen in the one who correctly worships God and gives Him His proper place. As godliness is exercised, brotherly kindness will be manifested. A right attitude toward God cannot help affecting one's attitude toward other people. As brotherly kindness ('phileo' love) is exercised, charity or love ('agape love') will ensue."[1]

The Proverbs lady is a pattern to follow in learning to show forth love and to accept love from others. Her testimony to her family and friends is that she excels.

PERSONAL APPLICATION

1. Look for ways to honestly compliment people around you. Remember, more is achieved through praise than criticism.

2. Ask God to develop a more loving attitude in your heart for family and friends.

3. Are you developing the Christian virtues listed in 2 Peter 1:5-7? God's strength is available to you to develop these qualities if you will ask Him.

4. Write a card or letter to a family member or perhaps a lonely senior citizen. Send an encouraging note to your pastor with well-chosen words of "silver."

5. "Love that seeks to do men good is cowardice when it refuses to prevent them from doing wrong"—Shailer Matthews.

LOVE'S ABC'S
You'll have your hands full and your heart filled trying to live out *Love's ABC's*.

Love Accepts, Behaves, Cheers, Defends, Enriches, Forgives, Grows, and Helps.

Love Includes, Joins, Kneels, Listens, Motivates, Notices, Overlooks, and Provides.

Love Quiets, Respects, Surprises, Tries, Understands, Volunteers, Warms, eXpects, and Yields.

Love in Action breaks the code that adds Zip in your life.

Stan Michaiski

(From *Pulpit Helps*)

NOTES

1. William G. Bellshaw, *Real Faith for Rough Times* (Denver: Accent Publications, 1978), 52.

Lesson 10

PATTERN FOR PRAISE

Favour is deceitful, and beauty is vain: but a woman that feareth the Lord, she shall be praised. Give her of the fruit of her hands; and let her own works praise her in the gates (Proverbs 31:30, 31).

A PATTERN WOMAN has a true perspective of values. She knows that it is easy to be deceived by favor or popularity and that beauty can be vain and shallow.

Favor (charm) and beauty are two characteristics most women seek. A woman of charm is pleasant to be with and a woman of beauty is refreshing to watch, but neither characteristic makes a woman of value. If charm is used to manipulate others, it then becomes deceitful. Impure actions may be lodged in a beautiful body resulting in temptations to others and the ruin of virtue and honor.

The crowning completion of the character of the Proverbs woman is that she "fears the Lord." With all her good qualities, she does not lack "one thing needful" for she is guided and governed by God's principles. This is the secret of her spotless character and her marvelous success. Her words, her ways, her dress and her household discipline are all ordered as in God's presence.

Others may pride themselves on their beauty or endeavor to obtain favor through winning words and pleasing manners. However, if there is no true character beyond such charms, the day will come when praise will give place to contempt. But the woman who fears God will be honored by all who appreciate virtue.

"Feareth the Lord" (Jehovah) means having a real sense of awe toward God. He is holy, omnipotent, omniscient and omnipresent; the list of divine attributes could go on indefinitely. He is all these things in their perfect, absolute state, and He deserves our homage and respect. He and His authority cannot be treated lightly. Yet, in the midst of all this holiness and majesty God is equally loving and forgiving. God is harsh in His judgment of sin but gentle in His treatment of penitent sinners. His love and forgiveness are readily available for those who confess their sin to Him and He washes their sin away as far as the east is from the west (Ps. 103:12).

Sadly enough, some people have difficulty accepting the freedom from guilt that God offers through His forgiveness—perhaps because they do not feel worthy. No one is worthy, but God grants His forgiveness just the same.

According to the dictionary, forgiveness is "to give up the wish to get even, or for revenge." Alexander Pope wrote many years ago, "To err is human, to forgive, divine."

Positionally, Christians are sinless and guiltless before God; however, they are still plagued by sin. Sins are committed every day, and Christians need to ask God for forgiveness. When this happens, God is not Judge but by restored fellowship is Father. Once forgiveness has been asked from God for a sin it need not be asked for again and again.

Lesson 1 suggested Bathsheba may be responsible for these instructions in Proverbs 31. If this is so, she is a pattern for forgiveness.

Read 2 Samuel chapter 11 and chapter 12:1-25. Much has been written about the weakness of King David as he indulged himself in the sin of adultery with Bathsheba. Some authors choose to leave Bathsheba blameless because any subject was obligated to obey the King. Other authors condemn her.

Eugenia Price in her book, *The Unique World of Women,*[1] suggests that King David's conscience was sensitive enough toward God to realize he needed forgiveness. David not only realized he had sinned, but his relationship to God was so vital that he recognized his sin was against God: "Against thee, thee only, have I sinned" (Ps. 51:4). As Nathan the prophet pointed the finger of conviction at David, he also assured the king of God's forgiveness, "The Lord also has put away your sin."

David knew God well enough to be able to accept God's forgiveness. Christ had not come yet and only a few men, mainly prophets of God, who received direct revelations from God understood the meaning of forgiveness. David, "a man after God's own heart," following the conviction of his guilt, asked and accepted God's forgiveness.

One reason Bathsheba might have shared a similar experience to David's of confessing the sin is that David's own walk with God after his sin with her was stronger and more vital than before. It does not seem logical that this spiritually sensitive man would have continued to love and respect Bathsheba if she had not entered into the cleansing forgiveness of God also.

Bathsheba was a beautiful woman outwardly. When Solomon was crowned king (1 Kings 2), her beauty had turned inward. A woman's inner beauty is dependent upon her relationship with God. Bathsheba permitted God to strengthen and beautify her inner life. She used her mistake as a guide to future, better conduct. She, like David, gave the sin over to God and permitted Him to forgive her. Bathsheba also forgave herself and went on to be a faithful help meet to David and a good mother. In Matthew 1:6, she is listed in the genealogy of Jesus Christ.

A woman today needs to accept God's forgiveness. Too often she will refuse to forgive herself, therefore in reality calling God a liar.

1. What do these verses tell about confession and forgiveness?

Psalm 32:5 _____

Proverbs 28:13 _____

Jeremiah 31:34 _____

Matthew 9:2 _____

Acts 5:31 _____

Acts 26:18 _____

1 John 1:9 _____

The burden of guilt for sin is removed by God; however, the

consequences of that sin often have to be dealt with. When a nail (sin) is removed from a wall or a board, the nail hole (consequence) is still in the wall. God does not remove the results of sin such as sickness due to drugs.

2. Read Psalm 51. David lists several steps to keep one from falling back into sin. List these steps.

Verse 6 _____

Verse 7 _____

Verse 8 _____

Verse 9 _____

Verse 10 _____

Verse 11 _____

Verse 12 _____

3. After these steps have been followed, what ministry will result?

Verse 13 _____

Verse 19 _____

Matthew Henry comments on verse 13: "David had been himself a transgressor, and therefore could speak experimentally to transgressors, and resolves, having himself found mercy with God in the way of repentance, to teach others God's ways, that is (1) Our way to God by repentance; he would teach others that had sinned to take the same course that he had taken, to humble themselves, to confess their sins, and seek God's face; and (2) God's way towards us in pardoning mercy; how ready He is to receive those that return to Him. He taught the former by his own example, for the direction of sinners in repenting; he taught the latter by his own experience, for their encouragement. By this psalm he is, and will be to the world's end, teaching transgressors, telling them what God had done for his soul. Penitents should be preachers.

"Secondly, what good effect he promises himself from his doing this: 'Sinners shall be converted unto thee'; and shall neither persist in their wanderings from Thee, nor despair of finding mercy in their returns to Thee. The great thing to be aimed at in teaching transgressors is their conversion to God; that is a happy point gained, and happy are those that are instrumental to contribute towards it."[2]

Verse 19 speaks of worship. Matthew Henry continues, "If God would show Himself reconciled to David and his people, as he had prayed, then they should go on with the public services of His house, (1) Cheerfully to themselves. The sense of God's goodness to them would enlarge their hearts in all the instances and express-ions of thankfulness and obedience. They will then come to His tabernacle with burnt-offerings, with whole burnt-offerings, which were intended purely for the glory of God, and they shall offer, not lambs and rams only, but bullocks, the costliest sacrifices upon His altar. (2) Acceptably to God 'Thou shalt be pleased with them.' It is a great comfort to a good man to think of the communion that is between God and His people in their public assemblies, how He is honored by their humble attendance on Him and they are happy in His gracious acceptance of it."[3]

John 8:1-11 records the account of the woman taken in adultery (wonder where the man was who was just as guilty?). The scribes and Pharisees did not care about the woman's embarrass-ment, they just used her as a "theological football." According to the law of Moses (Lev. 20:10; Deut. 22:22) the woman should have been stoned. The people tried to trick Jesus: "You say to love every-body, but the law says to stone her." Jesus began to write on the ground (possibly the Ten Commandments or the sins of those present) and when He was finished said, "He that is without sin among you, let him first cast a stone at her." Verse 9 says, "And they which heard it, being convicted by their own conscience, went out one by one, beginning at the eldest. . . ." As the accusers left, Jesus was alone with the woman and He asked her, "Where are those thine accusers? hath no man condemned thee?" She said, "No man, Lord." She had had enough punishment and failure. Listen to Jesus' words: "Neither do I condemn thee: go, and sin no more." Notice the simplicity of His command, "Go." Remove yourself from the temptation. "No more" means something is going to happen in the future that is not like what has ever happened in the past. Guilt or self-induced punishment need not be a part of life now. In the eyes of God a forgiven person is just as pure, virtuous and whole as if there had been no sin. The blood of Jesus Christ cleanses all sins. That is the miracle of the inexhaustible grace of God.

4. After confessing sin and accepting God's forgiveness, what encouragement is given in these verses?

Isaiah 43:18 _____

Isaiah 43:25 _____

Philippians 3:13, 14 _____

Forgetting "those things which are behind" is not always easy. This not only includes past failures but also past achievements. The human mind is such a fabulous computer with a permanent filing system called "memory" that it is doubtful one can fully forget the past. People do not really forget anything; however, some situations are better not remembered.

The dictionary definition of "forget" is "to lose (facts, etc.) from the mind; be unable to remember; to overlook . . . intentionally." In order to forget past hurts or failures (or achievements), God must do the erasing. Isaiah 54:4 records, "For thou shalt forget . . . and shalt not remember." God is the One who will take the place of painful memories and make the forgetting possible. Then the admonition is to "press toward the mark (goal)." Don't look back. Remember, today is the first day of the rest of your life.

Praise God for the privilege of knowing Him as Savior and the great gift He has given of this daily release from guilt through forgiveness and the "extra" supernatural gift of forgetting.

Some women are praised above what they deserve, but those who praise the Proverbs woman *"give her of the fruit of her hands."* They give her that which she has dearly earned and is justly due to her.

A tree is known by its fruit; therefore, if the fruit is good, it will be praised. The same is true of the fruit of the hands of a woman. If her children respect her and conduct themselves as they should, they demonstrate the fruit of her hands and she reaps the benefits because of the care she has given them.

5. What does 1 Timothy 5:4 instruct regarding children?

The Proverbs woman does not applaud herself but accepts praise from others. Her good works will proclaim her praise as her relatives and friends observe her. The widows gave the best praise of Dorcas when they showed the coats and garments she made for the poor (Acts 9:39).

6. What does Paul say in Romans 12:3? _____

_____

As mentioned earlier, the success of the pattern woman is her relationship with God. Today, women can draw upon this same Source by living a Spirit-controlled life. Beverly LaHaye in her book *The Spirit-Controlled Woman* [4] lists three steps to becoming a Spirit-controlled woman.

Receiving salvation by inviting the Lord Jesus Christ into your life (Rom. 10:13).

Live in the control of the Holy Spirit (Eph. 5:18; Rom. 8:5).

Read the Word of God. The results of a Spirit-controlled life are a joyful heart, a thankful spirit, and a submissive attitude (Col. 3:16-18; Eph. 5:18-21).

The Holy Spirit is a gentle Teacher. He leads Christians along as fast as they yield to His control. He is faithful to shed light on the dark areas of each life so that they may choose to yield to Him and continue to grow more like the Lord Jesus Christ; or Christians may choose not to yield—the choice is theirs.

7. What do the following verses instruct?

Romans 6:13 _____

Romans 6:16 _____

8. Was Jesus totally yielded to the Father (John 5:30)? _____

Yielding to the Holy Spirit involves a process of discipline.

In Galatians 5:16, Paul commands, "Walk in the Spirit." He also describes the conflict between Spirit and flesh in verses 17 and 18. He then goes on to contrast the two radically different lifestyles—that of walking in the Spirit or living in the flesh.

Some people can hide their sins of the flesh. However, as Thomas Watson wrote, "When men forbear vice, they do not hate it. There is no change of heart. Sin is curbed, it is not cured. A lion may be in chains, but he is a lion still."

Sin breaks down into four categories according to John Mac-Arthur: "Sexual, religious, human relationships and relationship to objects."[5] In Galatians 5:21, Paul says, "They which do (practice) such things shall not inherit the kingdom of God."

What happens if a Christian slips up and becomes angry, jealous, critical or has an immoral thought? "The Greek term for practice refers to something that is habitual, done over and over continually. Those who habitually do these things will not inherit the kingdom. The term 'kingdom of God' has reference to the completeness of salvation (Acts 28:31). Paul is indicating that believers habitually characterized by such deeds are not kingdom citizens. He is not saying that if a Christian does these things he is damned. Christians sin, but they are forgiven (1 John 1:9; 2:1). Christians sin, but they are restrained from habitual uninterrupted sinning by the working of the Spirit."[6]

Paul describes what Christians could be like with the Holy Spirit's power working in and through their lives in Galatians 5. He contrasts, "Now the works of the flesh are. . . . But the fruit of the Spirit is . . . ." (Gal. 5:19, 22).

M. R. DeHaan in his book, *Galatians,* comments, "Notice the two words, WORKS and FRUIT. Works of the flesh—Fruit of the Spirit. Works speaks of effort, mechanics, toils of labor. Works results in weariness, faintness, and other frustration. It is accompanied by much display and noise of hammers and saws. However, Fruit is the result of just receiving, yielding, and accepting. It means having no confidence in the flesh, but an honest confession of weakness, an earnest plea for forgiveness, and a surrender to the will of God."[7]

Before listing the Fruit of the Spirit, Paul catalogs the Works of the Flesh.

9. Read Galatians 5:18-21. What are the Works of the Flesh?

_____

_____

_____

These are the works of the old nature before a person has a personal relationship with Jesus Christ. Unfortunately, they will sneak into the life of a Christian occasionally. These works must be overcome by walking in the Spirit (Gal. 5:16), being led by the

Spirit (Gal. 5:18) and living in the Spirit (Gal. 5:25). By yielding to God, the Fruit of the Spirit is produced.

10. List the Fruit of the Spirit in Galatians 5:22, 23.

_____

_____

_____

These are not FRUITS but FRUIT. The "works" of the flesh are plural and Paul lists at least seventeen of them, but the "fruit" of the Spirit is singular and consists of these groups of virtues:

Relationship to self—personal fruit—love, joy, peace. These have to do with our own personal life.

Relationship to others—outreaching fruit—longsuffering, gentleness, goodness. This is our attitude of compassion toward others.

Relationship to God—up-reaching fruit—faith, meekness, temperance.

Nine parts of one fruit, all supplied by the Holy Spirit.

The Fruit of the Spirit could be compared to an orange—many sections, all making up one fruit as illustrated.

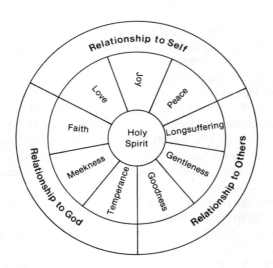

"Christian character is not mere moral or legal correctness, but the possession and manifestation of nine graces: love, joy, peace—character as an inward state; longsuffering, gentleness, goodness—character in expression toward man; faith, meekness, temperance—character in expression toward God. Taken together they present a moral portrait of Christ."[8]

Let us now take a more detailed look at the Fruit of the Spirit.

Relationship to Self

Love—Paul speaks here of agape, the highest form of love. Agape love is not emotion; it is self-sacrifice (John 15:13; Rom. 5:5).

Joy—refers to a heavenly joy; the joy of God passing through a Christian. Heavenly joy is based not on how well things are going but on God. Full joy is in relationship to God—the joy of Jesus given to Christians (John 15:11).

Peace—This kind of peace is a tranquility of mind based on a relationship to God. Like joy, it has nothing to do with circumstances. Peace is that inward calm confidence that no matter what happens, everything between a man (woman) and God is right. It is not being in peaceful circumstances but having a peaceful heart that counts (John 16:33; Phil. 4:7).

Relationship to Others

Longsuffering—or patience is a gentle tolerance of others, no matter how they treat us. It is often connected with mercy and is a virtue for the believer to pursue (2 Pet. 1:6). The source of this patience is the Holy Spirit (Col. 1:11).

Gentleness—or kindness means tenderness in view of the weakness of human personality and the depth of human need. A characteristic of God, this sympathetic gentleness does not imply weakness. It is directed toward others. This is gentleness wrapped in conviction, not milque-toast lack of conviction. James 3:17 says gentleness accompanies the wisdom that comes from above.

Goodness—means moral excellence, spiritual excellence. Romans 5:7 implies a difference between righteousness and goodness: "For scarcely for a righteous man will one die: yet peradventure for a good man some would even dare to die." Righteousness is following the standard. A righteous person would evict a widow for not paying her rent. Goodness would pay the bill for the widow. God is both righteous and good.

Relationship to God

Faith—or faithfulness means trustworthiness, loyalty, steadfastness. First Corinthians 4:2 says the servants of Christ should be found trustworthy.

Meekness—or gentleness is the only Fruit of the Spirit that is not characteristic of God the Father, because it means "humble, submissive to the divine will." Meekness was, however, a characteristic of Jesus Christ. It is a form of humility. In the New Testament, meekness is used to describe submissiveness to the will of God (Matt. 5:5); teachableness (James 1:21); and consideration for others (1 Cor. 4:21).

Temperance—or self-control is the ability to keep yourself in check. One of many commands in Scripture is in 2 Peter 1:6 where we are instructed to add self-control to our faith. As we walk in the Spirit and He controls us, self-control is sure to be there too.

The totality of the Fruit of the Spirit is commanded of the believer, exemplified in Jesus Christ and produced by the Holy Spirit. Galatians 5:23 instructs, "Against such [things] there is no law." Because God gave His Spirit, a truly beautiful woman will demonstrate the Fruit of the Spirit in her life as she walks consistently and obediently.

To be sensitive to the leading of the Holy Spirit, a woman must have a daily devotional life by spending time studying the Bible and by spending time in prayer. Just as a woman's physical body requires daily sustenance, so must she have spiritual food for nourishment and development. Evidence of Christian maturity is a desire to study God's Word and to know Him better; to understand and obey His commandments; to seek out and claim His promises.

Share David's talk with the Lord in Psalm 119:1-50. Notice his reverence for that part of the Scriptures to which he had access.

11. Read John 1:1. Who is being referred to as God's "Word"?

When a woman loves Jesus Christ, she loves the Word, because He is the Word. By reading and meditating on the Scriptures illuminated by the Holy Spirit, she is making God's written truth a part of herself. Jesus Christ is not the Bible, which is also referred to as the Word, but He is God's living expression of truth.

12. Was the Word of God important to the Children of Israel (Deut. 8:3)? _____

13. How was it important to Jesus (Luke 4:4)? _____

_____

14. What did David say in Psalm 119:105? _____

_____

15. What admonition does Paul give in 2 Timothy 2:15? _____

_____

16. For what purpose has Scripture been given according to 2 Timothy 3:17? _____

_____

_____

17. What effects will the Word of God produce in our lives?

Psalm 119:11 _____

Romans 10:17 _____

Hebrews 4:12 _____

1 Peter 1:23 _____

18. Name the attitudes toward the Word of God we should possess as listed in Psalm 119:11-18. _____

_____

19. What commands are given in Deuteronomy 6:6, 7? _____

_____

Prayer is to a woman's spiritual life as breath is to her physical life. A formula to follow for a daily prayer life is ACTS—Adoration, Confession, Thanksgiving and Supplication.

A - Adoration is worship of God. What do these verses say?

Matthew 4:10 _____

John 4:23 _____

    C · *Confession* of sin is necessary to keep the channels of prayer open.

Psalm 19:12 _____

Psalm 26:2 _____

1 John 1:8-10 _____

_____

    T · *Thanksgiving* to God is a must as indicated in these verses:

Psalm 100:4 _____

Psalm 147:7 _____

Ephesians 5:20 _____

Colossians 3:17 _____

    S · *Supplication* is making our requests known to God.

1 Timothy 2:1, 2 _____

Ephesians 6:18 _____

Matthew 7:7, 8 _____

John 15:7 _____

Adoration is concerned with the worship of God; confession with our faults; thanksgiving with blessings and supplication with needs.

Another formula to remember in becoming *"a woman that feareth the Lord"* and to receive God's praise is to MATURE in the Christian life:

    M · Meet God in daily prayer (Eph. 6:18).

    A · Allow time each day for reading the Bible (Acts 17:11).

    T · Turn every moment of your life over to God in obedience (John 14:21).

    U · Understand you are to witness daily by words and actions (1 Pet. 3:15).

    R · Rejoice that the Holy Spirit is in your life, indwelling and empowering you (Acts 1:8).

    E · Enjoy your Christian experience (Prov. 16:20).

When a woman develops her inner beauty by spending time reading the Word of God and praying, she will learn the fine art of victorious Christian living through the Holy Spirit working in her life.

The Proverbs woman is rewarded here and hereafter as verse 31 states: *"her own works praise her in the gates."* What greater praise and reward could she desire in this life than the consciousness that she has done her best for her Savior? What greater reward could she ask after leaving this world than the happy privilege of living and reigning throughout the ceaseless ages of eternity with her Savior, the Lord Jesus Christ? She will enjoy the beautiful city, the fellowship of dear ones, the heavenly music and more; but the joy and thrill of the ages will be to see Jesus and to be like Him forever.

Today, in light of the New Testament revelation, verse 31 has more than a hint of the coming manifestation of the judgment seat of Christ. When the pride, folly and iniquity of this earth are past, the woman who has been described in Proverbs 31 will appear in her Lord's presence with rejoicing, bearing her sheaves with her. At His feet she will cast down the fruit of her hands and the works His grace has produced in and through her. How sweet to hear His words of praise in the gate: "Well done, thou good and faithful servant: thou hast been faithful over a few things . . . enter thou into the joy of thy lord" (Matt. 25:21).

With this last verse, the pattern is completed for ladies. This pattern fits all shapes and sizes. When used, ladies' adorning will be found to praise, honor and glorify Jesus Christ at His appearing.

PERSONAL APPLICATION

1. Remember to forgive others as God forgives you (Matt. 6:15). *Freedom of Forgiveness* by David Augsburger might be helpful.

2. Memorize Galatians 5:22, asking the Lord to help you develop this Fruit of the Spirit in your daily living.

3. Through "ACTS" you can become a "MATURE" Christian woman.

NOTES

1. Eugenia Price, *The Unique World of Women* (Grand Rapids: Zondervan Publishing House, 1969), 77.

2. Henry, *Commentary on the Whole Bible,* 434.

3. Ibid., 435, 436.

4. Beverly LaHaye, *Spirit-Controlled Woman* (LaHabra, CA: Harvest House Publishers, 1976), 170.

5. John MacArthur, Jr., *Galatians, Liberated for Life* (Glendale, CA: Gospel Light Publications, 1976), 110, 111.

6. Ibid.

7. M. R. DeHaan, *Galatians* (Grand Rapids: Radio Bible Class, 1960), 166, 167.

8. C. I. Scofield, *The Scofield Reference Bible* (New York: Oxford University Press, 1909), 1247.

CONCLUSION

The pattern displayed in Proverbs 31, designed by divine inspiration, begins with a *"a virtuous woman"* and completes the pattern with a *"woman that feareth the Lord."* For the lovely features described—her fidelity to her husband, her active personal habits, her good management and diligence in her family, her consideration for the necessities and comforts of others, her watchfulness of conduct, her tenderness for the poor and afflicted, her kind and courteous behavior to all—this completeness of character and grace could only flow from that virtue which is identified with vital godliness. Such virtue is the good fruit that proves the tree to be good according to Matthew 7:17: "Even so every good tree bringeth forth good fruit; but a corrupt tree bringeth forth evil fruit."

The virtuous woman does not seek the praise of men. She is content to be known and loved within her own circles and never pushes herself into being noticed. However, as a public blessing she cannot be hid (Acts 9:39). All will say, *"Give her of the fruit of her hands; and let her own works praise her in the gates."* Some women are known for their nobleness of stock because of their family heritage, others for their fortune and others for their beauty; however, the Proverbs lady is known by the deeds she herself has done and her own works declare her excellent worth.

Through this pattern lady it is observed that a woman's relationship to God and her earthly duties go hand in hand. A woman should be scrupulously exact in all her household obligations, in everything within her realm of responsibility, being careful not to bring reproach upon her holy profession because of negligence (Titus 2:1-5). She should not be careless or slovenly, putting her important duties out of time and place. The summing up of her practical duties is that she has "diligently followed every good work" (1 Tim. 5:10).

A valuable guide for the choice of a marriage partner is another pattern provided from Proverbs 31. Let virtue, not beauty, be the primary object— *"a woman that feareth the Lord."* This is the solid basis for happiness. A quote from *The Commentary on Proverbs* by Charles Bridges, regarding selection of a marriage partner, is "If I choose her for her beauty, I shall love her no longer than while that continues; and then farewell at once both duty and delight. But if I love her for her virtues; then, though all other sandy foundations fail, yet will my happiness remain entire."[1] The godly choice is stamped with the seal of divine acceptance.

Through this study from Proverbs 31 women are given a pattern to follow, a guide, a model and a goal to aim toward. As Jesus said in Luke 10:37, "Go, and do thou likewise."

NOTES

1. Bridges, *The Commentary on Proverbs,* 628.

BIBLIOGRAPHY

Bridges, Charles. *The Commentary on Proverbs*. Carlisle, PA: The Banner of Truth Trust, 1846.

Brooks, Keith L. *Christian Character*. Chicago: Moody Bible Institute, 1961.

Campus Crusade for Christ, International. *The Christian and Stewardship*. Arrowhead Springs, CA: n.d.

DeHaan, M. R. *Galatians*. Grand Rapids: Radio Bible Class, 1960.

Erdman, Joy. *Pattern for Living*. Crown Point, IN: Christian Womanhood, 1977.

Ford, Alvy E. *The Bible in Verse*. Lincoln, NE: Back to the Bible Publishers, 1955.

Goodboy, Eadie. *God's Daughter*. Edmonds, WA: Aglow Publications, 1974.

Handford, Elizabeth Rice. *Your Clothes Say It For You*. Murfreesboro, TN: Sword of the Lord Publishers, 1976.

Hunter, Emily. *Christian Charm Course*. Portland, OR: Manna Publications, 1967.

Instant Sewing. New York: Graphic Enterprises, Inc., 1968.

Ironside, H. A. *Notes on the Book of Proverbs*. New York: Loizeaux Brothers, 1908.

Jensen, Irving J. *Proverbs*. Chicago: Moody Bible Institute, 1976.

Keil, C. F. and Delitzsch, F. *Commentary on the Old Testament*. Grand Rapids: Wm. B. Eerdmans Publishing Co., 1975.

LaHaye, Beverly. *Spirit-Controlled Woman*. LaHabra, CA: Harvest House Publishers, 1976.

Landorf, Joyce. *The Fragrance of Beauty*. Wheaton, IL: Victor Books, 1973.

Lewis, Clifford. *God's Ideal Woman*. Murfreesboro, TN: Sword of the Lord Publishers, 1941.

Lockyer, Herbert. *All the Women of the Bible*. Grand Rapids: Zondervan Publishing Co., 1967.

MacArthur, John, Jr. *Galatians, Liberated for Life*. Glendale, CA: Gospel Light Publications, 1976.

Miller, Ella Mae. *The Joy of Housekeeping*. Old Tappan, NJ: Fleming H. Revell, 1975.

_____ . "Problems Working Mothers Face." Harrison, VA: Heart to Heart, n.d.

Navigators. *Lessons on Christian Living.* Colorado Springs, CO: NavPress.

Ockenga, Harold J. *Women Who Made Bible History.* Grand Rapids: Zondervan Publishing House, 1962.

Orr, James. *International Standard Bible Encyclopedia.* Grand Rapids: Wm. B. Eerdmans Publishing Co., 1939.

Palmer, Elmer. *So A Child May Understand.* Eaton, CO: First Baptist Church, 1966.

Rice, Shirley. *The Christian Home.* Norfolk, VA: Norfolk Christian Schools, 1965.

Roper, Gayle G. *Wife, Mate, Mother, Me!* Grand Rapids: Baker Book House, 1975.

Strong, James. *The Exhaustive Concordance of the Bible.* Grand Rapids: Wm. B. Eerdmans Publishing Company, 1964.

The Amplified Bible. Grand Rapids: Zondervan Publishing Co., 1965.

The New American Standard Bible. LaHabra, CA: The Lockman Foundation, 1960.

The Ryrie Study Bible. Chicago: Moody Press, 1976.

The Scofield Reference Bible. New York: Oxford University Press, 1909.

U.S Bureau of th ensus. *Statistical Abstract of the United States, 1983.* Washington, D.C., 1984.

Young, Robert. *Analytical Concordance to the Bible.* Grand Rapids: Wm. B. Eerdmans Publishing Co., 1964.